A HEART
THAT WILL
NEVER HEAL

Based on a True Story

MARGARET JEFFERSON

A Heart That Will Never Heal

For information contact:

margaretjeffersoninspires@gmail.com

ISBN:

979-8-9911309-0-5 (paperback)

979-8-9911309-1-2 (hardback)

Second Edition: October 2024

Preface

"YOU'RE NOT A VICTIM FOR
SHARING YOUR STORY. YOU ARE A
SURVIVOR SETTING THE WORLD ON
FIRE WITH YOUR TRUTH. AND YOU
NEVER KNOW WHO NEEDS YOUR
LIGHT, YOUR WARMTH, AND
RAGING COURAGE."

.

-ALEX ELLE

At the time I decided to write this book, I was alone in the house due to the pandemic. I often had something to do or somewhere to go, but now I was all alone with my thoughts.

I had been running from my thoughts for years and finally had to come to terms with my past. I began to speak to God about my pain and even became ill in my body. I began to think about what I would leave behind if I were to die tomorrow. I decided to start writing so that I could tell my story in hopes of encouraging and uplifting others. This book discusses many stages in my life. The stages include the joys of falling in love with someone and the disappointments. I also discuss the factors of being a grieving mother after the death of my only child, facing the judgment and opinions of others, and dealing with the hurt and anger. I also cover failed relationships and people sabotaging certain dynamics to try to prevent me from reaching my dreams and goals. I've realized that, through all the challenges, God was always there and never left my side. I am thankful that I can encourage and uplift someone and let them know that, despite their challenges, they should never give up. We only get one life, so walk in your purpose.

Contents

Introduction

"THERE IS NO GREATER AGONY
THAN BEARING AN UNTOLD STORY
INSIDE YOU."

-Maya Angelou

"1 in 4 women and 1 in 10 men experience sexual violence, physical violence and/or stalking by an intimate partner during their lifetime with Intimate Partner Violence IPV- related impact such as being concerned for their safety, PTSD symptoms, injury, or needing victim services." — National Coalition Against Domestic Violence (NCADV)

Acc+ording to the Department of Justice (DOJ), physical abuse "involves hitting, slapping, shoving, grabbing, pinching, biting, hair pulling. This type of abuse also includes denying a partner medical care or forcing alcohol and/or drug use upon him or her."

The DOJ says that sexual abuse is "coercing or attempting to coerce any sexual contact or behavior without consent. Sexual abuse includes, but is certainly not limited to, marital rape, attacks on sexual parts of the body, forcing sex after physical violence has occurred, or treating one in a sexually demeaning manner."

The DOJ describes emotional/verbal abuse as "undermining an individual's sense of self-worth and/or self-esteem...This may include, but is not limited to constant criticism, diminishing one's abilities, name-calling, or damaging one's relationship with his or her children." Verbal abuse often involves yelling, put-downs, name- calling, and belittling behaviors."

The DOJ defines economic abuse as "controlling

or restraining a person's ability to acquire, use, or maintain economic resources to which they are entitled. This includes using coercion, fraud, or manipulation to restrict a person's access to money, assets, credit, or financial information; unfairly using a person's personal economic resources, including money, assets, and credit, or exerting undue influence over a person's financial and economic behavior or decisions, including forcing default on joint or other financial obligations, exploiting powers of attorney, guardianship, or conservatorship, or failing or neglecting to act in the best interests of a person to whom one has a fiduciary duty."

The DOJ calls technology abuse "an act or pattern of behavior that is intended to harm, threaten, control, stalk, harass, impersonate, exploit, extort, or monitor another person that occurs using any form of technology, including but not limited to: internet enabled devices, online spaces and platforms, computers, mobile devices, cameras and imaging programs, apps, location tracking devices, or communication technologies, or any other emerging technologies."

They describe psychological abuse as follows: "elements of psychological abuse include—but are not limited to—causing fear by intimidation; threatening physical harm to self, partner, children, or partner's family or friends; destruction of pets and property; and forcing isolation from family, friends, or school and/or work."

I wanted to ask God why all of these things were happening to me, but I was told to never question God.

Figure It Out

> "I HAVE SURVIVED. I AM HERE. CONFUSED, SCREWED UP, BUT HERE. SO HOW CAN I FIND MY WAY? IS THERE A CHAIN SAW OF THE SOUL. AN AX I CAN TAKE TO MY MEMORIES OR FEARS?"
>
> -Laurie Halse Anderson

I never imagined that this would happen to me. I was bloody, my clothes were torn, I was screaming for help, and people watched in disbelief, not knowing what to do because they had never seen a sight like this. I was in the middle of the street crying for help. I was halfway naked, with only a ripped, gray sparkling top and black bra on top and the lower part of my body completely exposed. I looked around in disarray, confused, lost, and trying to understand what was happening. I was trying to find a car that resembled a sign for help. I was in the middle of the street as cars passed by. My bloody hands reached for the handle of a white car that resembled a security vehicle. The women drove off rapidly. People were coming from all over looking at me, but I was worried about my son. At that moment my mother spider sense went off. This is one of the sixth senses that mothers have for their children when they are in trouble. In the midst of losing blood and feeling lightheaded, as if I were going to pass out, I continued to search for someone to help my son. As I walked tirelessly for what seemed like an eternity searching for help, I found an officer to help me. I would later find out his name was Officer Scott.

I stood across the street, bloody, tired, and

helpless, waiting for the ambulance to arrive. People continuously crowded around me, wondering how, what, when, and why, but I could not focus on the people around me. The only thing I could think about was my concern for my son. I lived in the hood; it seemed like the ambulance took longer to come to that area, although the hospital was not far. The ambulance finally arrived. I then saw my mom look into it with concern. I could see her oval face and high cheekbones that framed her mid-length, salt-and-pepper hair and brown complex skin. Her rounded eyes looked around with concern. She called my name as the ambulance door closed; I could see my neighbor talking to her and letting her know that I was hurt and in danger. I saw another stretcher in the back. I could hear the EMTs whispering, saying there were two people. Before they drove off, I heard them say another ambulance would come to pick him up. I was asking, "Where is my baby? Get my baby. Where is my baby?" They were telling me to calm down. How could I calm down when I didn't know where my child was? I was in a panic. My hands were sweating, and my heart was beating rapidly. I was wondering how I got like this. What was happening?

Things were not always like this. I was just a regular girl from the West Side of Chicago. My name is Malina. I am a dark-skinned, petite girl with a round face, almond- shaped eyes, mid-length hair, and a beautiful smile. I had lived on the West Side of Chicago all my life, so this was all I knew. Most of the people in the neighborhood were friends who later became family. We looked out for each other. I mean, it had its ups and downs, but it was not what everyone portrayed Chicago to be. I was used to the loud music playing across the street at the gas station and loud talking. This was normal to me. It was loud, and there was always something going on. I knew the other things that went on in my neighborhood from drugs to violence and alcoholism. I was sheltered by my parents and would go to church four times out of the week. I was not allowed to talk to boys but would sneak and try to hang out when I could.

I can remember going to the Circle. You are probably wondering what the Circle is? It was a great hangout that everyone would go to in the hood. Everyone knew that all the guys with the rims and cars were going to be there. You could really chill and walk around and meet different people. My friends and I would hang out all night if we could. I had just graduated from high school and was trying to find my way as a young adult. I would get guys' numbers and sometimes call and would go out on dates, but nothing serious. Most of the guys were entertaining multiple females or just wanted to have sex, but I was searching for something more.

I went on a blind date with my cousin and met a guy. She needed me to be her wing woman, and I really didn't want to go. Being that she was one of my favorite cousins, I decided to help her out. The guy's name was Steven; he was short and dark skinned, with a low-cut fade and nice teeth. We met at the AMC theater in Melrose Park. We all decided to go to IHOP and finished talking, getting to know each other. I really enjoyed myself and wanted to hang out again. Little did I know that he would be in my life for what would seem like forever. He was an extremely nice guy and really liked me. I was eighteen when I met him. The relationship with this guy did not work out, because I was naïve and young at the time, but we later developed a strong friendship. When I was growing up, the media would show women that it was cool to talk to multiple guys. I tried to mimic the women I saw on TV and who were often portrayed in my community. "You are young; date multiple people," they said. "You can settle down when you get older." I always wanted that fairy-tale type of relationship that I would see on TV. I never had a guy that splurged on me like the other girls. I always wanted someone to like me enough to treat me like that special girl. My mom taught me to always have my own and never depend on a man. At that time in my life, I really did not know the full capacity of how to be in a relationship and how a man should treat me. Although I came from a loving, two-parent household, I was still trying to piece things together. I had two brothers but often referred to friends for guidance, like any teenage girl. I was trying to figure out how life worked.

I was young, vibrant, and free, but always wanted more. My friends and I had fun going to concerts, meeting new guys, and doing what we wanted. I did not have any children at the time and was free to go. I enjoyed the carefree life, but I was missing something—a relationship. I yearned for someone to love me and to establish a real relationship— a companion. I wanted that perfect love story that you see in the movies. Guess I was a hopeless romantic.

I met the next guy. Let's just call him Charlie. I remember that when I first met him, I was nineteen years old. Charlie was three years older than me, but I could handle someone older. I talked to guys but had never been in a full- blown relationship.

Charlie was who I had been praying for, but little did I know that it would turn into a nightmare. A nightmare that I would never be able to wake up from. I will never forget Charlie for as long as I live; I have the scars on my body and heart to prove it.

I do not even know where to begin. I can remember it like it was yesterday; I was invited to Charlie's cousin Shelia's birthday party. I knew her through mutual friends. It was February 2006, a couple of days after Valentine's Day. Still single, I did not have a valentine. I decided to wear my burgundy jacket with pink stripes on the side with a white tee and blue jeans with my crisp, white Reeboks. I had just gotten my hair done with a long, flowing, curly extension to frame my round face. You couldn't tell me nothing; I knew I looked good.

I arrived at the party. There were not many people— mostly her family and a couple of friends. I went to the back of the house, to the kitchen, to get some food. To my surprise there were two guys around my age in the kitchen as well. We glanced at each other as I walked back into the dining area. Charlie's cousin Shelia stated that he was interested and wanted to get to know me. I was a little feisty back then, so I said, "Okay, where is he at? If he wants to talk to me, he needs to come to me." He then came from the kitchen area and introduced himself. "Hi, my name is Charlie." He was a tall, light-skinned man with a chiseled face, round, mesmerizing eyes, and a low-cut fade with waves in his hair. I stated my name and said, "Well, Charlie, you can get my plate and walk me home." He walked me to my house, which was four or five houses away. We exchanged numbers, and the rest is history. We were together almost every day. Either I was over his house, or he was at my house. We talked on the phone for hours. It was love that I was feeling, and I loved it. This is exactly what I had been praying for. It was only one and a half weeks, but it seemed like we had known each other forever. We started having sex—I know what you are thinking:

that's kind of quick. At least it was with one person, and now we were a couple. I later noticed that Charlie had a temper and would have spurts of anger. I now know that if a man cannot take accountability for his actions, you need to run—and I mean fast. We got past that hurdle in our relationship and were trying to work on us. He was so sweet to me and would buy me things and enjoyed being with me. It was not all about sex with Charlie; it was different. He wanted to be with me and only me. I was really falling for him fast. This was a wonderful feeling that I never wanted to end.

Charlie was on probation at the time and had to be in at a certain time. I did not know much about the law and how it really worked, but I would later find out the ins and outs of the system. I was naïve and lived in the community, where it was common to talk to the block boys. Block boys are the guys that normally sell drugs on the street corners. This was normal where I lived, but little did I know it was a different world that I was unaware of. Charlie was almost off probation, meaning we would have more time to spend with each other. He also had a five-year-old son from a previous relationship. I was nineteen and about to turn twenty years old; I did not know much about being a stepmom, but I was willing to try. He would always tell me they were a package deal, and I had to respect that, which I did. He was three years older than me and had a lot of responsibilities. He did not work but lived with his parents in the suburbs. They had a nice home and cars. This was new scenery for me, and it made me disregard any of his flaws. I was from the hood, where I wasn't used to seeing and being around this kind of environment, so it was a new venture for me. I was in awe of Charlie and his put-together family. I had always wished my family would be close-knit instead of scattered and in our own worlds. It seemed like Charlie had the best life, and I was eager to be a part of this family dynamic.

It seemed like Charlie had everything I was looking for. It felt like a fairy tale. I would often drive his mom's truck and show it off to my friends. I felt like I was a part of his family, and we were going in the right direction. I loved him and really wanted to be there for him, and he loved me too. We would spend quality time together daily, going to the park, the movies, and family gatherings. I had never felt this way before; I had butterflies every time we were together. If this is what love consisted of, I wanted to be in this moment forever. I enjoyed the attention of being the only one and finally being in a committed relationship. It was no games, just us—or so I thought.

It was Charlie's birthday. I was so excited his family decided to throw him a surprise birthday party, and they wanted to know if I would like to pitch in. I said, "Sure." I had decided to buy Charlie the newest Timberland boots to surprise him. I just knew he would love them. The party started at 7:00 p.m., and he was supposed to pick me up from my house for what I thought was a family gathering. I contacted Charlie by phone, but it was going to voicemail. I hoped everything was okay. It was 7:30 p.m. when he picked up to say that he was on his way. Okay, what a relief. Everything was good. It was now 9:00 p.m., and Charlie still had not arrived and was not answering his phone. He finally arrived at 9:30 p.m. At this point I was upset and ready to curse him out. I got to the party, and everyone's faces looked as if they knew something that I did not. I later found out that he had taken his child's mother to the party first, and then he came to get me. He made up an excuse that he had to pick up his son and take his ex to the store, and they went to the family gathering. I know looking back that I was so naive. I felt so stupid. We later made up, and I was hoping we could go back to that happy place we were once at. I was so wrong. I did not know, but we would never get back to that precise happy place ever again. Then I thought the bad times had passed, and it was back to us.

The next day I asked Charlie to drop off a friend for me since he had to drop off his son at his mother's house; he agreed. I did not think anything of it. He decided to drop off his son first because that would be closer. What was so bad about that, right? Actually my friend reported that he was flirting and having physical contact with the mother of his child. I could not believe what she was saying, even after he and I had finally decided to work on our relationship again. So many thoughts and emotions fluttered through me at that time. I felt a pit in my stomach. I was about to become sick, because I had never loved someone the way I loved Charlie. Why would he do this to me? What did she have that I didn't? Was she prettier than me? What was wrong with me? Why didn't Charlie love me anymore? After hearing this devastating news, I had come to my senses—Charlie had to go. I practiced the next couple of days as to how I was going to break up with him. What would I say to him? I ignored his calls for two days. He called my house and cell phone what seemed to be fifty times. I thought that he called so much because he really missed me, not knowing that this wasn't normal. I just was not ready to talk to him. The day finally came. I stated, "I think we need to talk." Those are the words that anyone would dread.

Charlie met me at my house, and I came out to the hallway. I stated, "I don't think this is going to work. I think you should be with the mother of your child." He became enraged. I had never seen him like that. Sure, we would argue, but nothing to this extent. He then raised his hand and slapped me in my face. I was stunned by this and began to cry and try to get away. In response to my attempts to fight back, Charlie raised his fist and punched me multiple times in my face. I began to cry uncontrollably. My parents heard the commotion and ran down the stairs. My mom tried to punch Charlie in his face to get him off me. My dad then came and pushed him out the door. Charlie fled the scene. I was in shock and in disbelief. I was shaking. My heart cracked into pieces at that moment. I could not believe this was happening to me. My godmother and Charlie's cousin Shelia stayed in the same building. My mother called my godmother and told her what had happened. She and Shelia came down the street to check on me. The police were called, and I pressed charges. I went to the hospital to make sure I didn't have any head injuries. While at the hospital, the nurse asked me if I was pregnant. I said, "No. I'm not pregnant." Or was I? I hadn't had my period, but I had spotted, so I was good. I didn't want to think about that at the time. I just wanted to make sure that there were not any major issues with my skull or anything. Everything was good, which made me relieved, but my face was swollen. I asked my friend if she could pick up a pregnancy test. I took it, and it came back inconclusive. I could not be pregnant, especially not by him after what he'd done. The next day I purchased two more tests. I just needed to know. Both came back positive. I did not want to be pregnant by him. "Why me, Lord?" I thought. I was conflicted about what I should do. Should I keep my baby or get an abortion? My family did not believe in abortions. Some family members were saying not to have the baby under those circumstances. I had some that said I should have the baby.

I finally decided to talk to my sister Sandra about what decision I should make. Sandra was dark skinned with short hair a medium build and tall with an oval-shaped face; she had beautiful chestnut eyes. I talked to her about having my baby and was crying to her. Sandra sat up on the bed with a cigarette halfway on her lips. She said, "You're not the first person to have a baby." I just looked at her like, "Really, that's your advice? I am crying my eyes out, and that is all you can say. Thanks for the help." I felt hurt and scared, knowing that I was carrying another life inside of me. I was confused and overwhelmed with feelings. I couldn't think and did not know what to do after all of this. My head was in a whirlwind. I wanted to hide away from everyone. Another issue was whether I should let Charlie know that he was about to be a father again. Decisions—decisions that I had to make.

I continued to pray and asked God for a sign and to provide me with guidance about what I should do.

I was attending Wilbur Wright Junior College for my associate's degree in art at that time and wondered if I would have to give up school. I was taking a class that focused on the human body and its various functions. I had to meet with my cohort at the museum to see an exhibit called Body Works where people had donated their bodies to science. At that moment I realized that this was my sign from God. I saw a pregnant mother whose body was donated to science. The exhibit displayed a fully developed and deceased baby inside of her uterus. I saw the different stages of the dead fetus from six weeks to nine months, documenting the process in which the baby had developed. It was at that moment that I decided I wanted to keep my baby. I wanted my baby to have life despite all the chaos.

I remember going to the doctor's office in the hood by myself, feeling lost and alone. I felt like another statistic. I felt like I was another black woman whose child would grow up without a father. I felt disappointed at the direction that my life was going in. I hated the way my life was turning out. I took the next semester off to focus on getting my life together. This was my life—pregnant and alone, out of school, unemployed, and on government assistance. I was trying to better my life and get out of the neighborhood, but I was back in the same cycle. I felt like a hamster on a wheel going in a circle; I felt I could not evolve, although I continued to try. I felt like a failure.

I had to go to the neighborhood doctor that accepted my medical card. Living in a low-income neighborhood, people had their way of treating minorities, without respect and without empathy, because we were less fortunate. The doctor in the neighborhood was horrible and would not provide me with the sufficient care I needed for my health. The only thing the doctor would state was not to wear flip-flops while pregnant. That was my doctor's visit. He got paid, and that's all I was told. I was thinking to myself, Great. I was one month into my pregnancy and was unaware as to what services were needed, but I knew it should be more than that. I guess that was the care you received for being on public aid. I wished I had someone to go through this pregnancy with me.

I later found out that my sister Sandra and her four friends were all pregnant. We called ourselves the fantastic five—like, what were the odds that we would all be pregnant together? Sandra and I began going to doctor's appointments together. Like I said earlier, the doctor was horrible. Months had passed since my first visit, so I asked for another ultrasound since I was further in my pregnancy. I could not believe that the doctor refused to provide me with a referral to receive another one. I informed him that I was unable to take the prenatal vitamin pills that he prescribed and was constantly gagging to swallow them, so I requested chewable prenatal vitamins. I could not believe that he disregarded my concerns and stated that it was "all in my head" and that he could not give me any other type of prenatal vitamins. Once again this was the treatment that I received for being on public aid. I wondered how many other clients were going through this. Sandra and I were tired of just being told not to wear flip-flops, having our health disregarded and being shown that he clearly did not care about our unborn babies. Sandra and I decided to search for another doctor. We could not take the lack of treatment from this one anymore.

I finally found another doctor willing to accept the medical card in the neighborhood. I did not know about other services outside of the neighborhood and was only familiar with what was nearby. I was six months pregnant and trying to figure it out.

The new doctor informed me that I needed to take a glucose test and other tests that were not provided by the previous doctor. I was also finally able to receive another ultrasound, along with chewable prenatal vitamins. I was finally getting the treatment that I needed for my unborn child and not being discriminated against.

It had been months, and I still had not talked to

31

Charlie or even let him know that I was pregnant. I was still in disbelief that he had hit me and placed me in this situation so that I had to press charges against him. The date finally arrived, and I had to go to court. I had to see Charlie. I was nervous, because I had never been in a situation like this, and I had not seen him since the altercation. Sandra always had my back, and she accompanied me as I went into the building for court. I decided to bring the ultrasound. I was told by an officer while checking into the court building to remove my dark black sunglasses. I was already embarrassed by the situation, but I had to remove my sunglasses and show my black eye for the whole world to see. I went into the courtroom and placed my sunglasses back on. As I entered the courtroom, I was told, once again, to remove my sunglasses. I tried to explain that I had a black eye. The officer stated, "It's not like we have never seen a black eye before." So insensitive, I thought to myself. I was already feeling stupid for dropping the charges because I had found out that I was pregnant and did not want the father of my child to be locked away. I stood in front of the judge ashamed, embarrassed, and feeling stupid. My emotions were bottled up. As I looked at the judge, I stated, "I want to drop the charges." As I left the courtroom, I saw Charlie talking to Sandra. She handed him the ultrasound and let him know that I was pregnant. He looked at me and repeatedly stated that he was sorry. I told him, "Okay," but continued to keep my distance.

Charlie knew all my weaknesses, because we had hung out every day before this situation. I am a spiritual person, and I believed that God would work things out. Charlie encouraged me to speak to his uncle who was a pastor. I decided to speak with him; he stated, "God said to forgive." I thought about it and decided to slowly start trusting Charlie. Looking back, I realize that Charlie never really took accountability for his actions. I never took accountability for accepting this type of behavior and was not being treated as a queen. I realize now that you can accept a person's behavior or leave the situation. You can love a person but should not be limited to dealing with being disrespected. I know now that is a red flag, and you should run and never look back. At that time, I didn't run. I continued to look forward in hopes that we could be a family. I was slowly becoming smitten with Charlie again. It was the honeymoon phase, and we were always together. He showed how much he loved me. After months and getting closer to my due date, I was back in love with Charlie.

I decided that I wanted to have a baby shower. I wanted to have it close to my home, since my parents had to rely on public transportation. I was also in my last month and did not think it was safe to drive a long distance to his parents' home, which was an hour away from mine. None of Charlie's family attended my baby shower, which made me unhappy. I felt hurt but had always thought that Charlie's mother had never liked me anyway. I felt like Charlie's father was more open and receptive than his mother. His father had passed but seemed like a nice guy for the short time I'd known him. My sister helped with the baby shower. I worked at Home Depot as a cashier. I had to pick up heavy items to scan, which was becoming difficult to do. I was having problems standing for long periods and was becoming dizzy while working, so I took an unpaid leave of absence. I did not have much money. My best friend at the time was also assisting with the baby shower, but we got into a stupid disagreement about a fruit tray. She stated that she was trying to help me and did not have to do anything. I was so upset and told her that she didn't have to come or do anything. I still hate it when people throw things that they do for you in your face. I was so hurt and upset by the situation.

My sister Sandra and I decided to get her Link card (food stamps) to buy some food. I spent whatever money that I had to set up my baby shower. Charlie came for a moment with his cousin. I just did not feel accepted by some of his family members. At that time I was a people pleaser. I was always wondering why someone didn't like me. What had I done? What could I do to make them like me? Today, I could care less. I felt like Charlie and I were getting closer, though. I knew the baby coming would provide me with that same fairy-tale story that every girl dreamed about—having a family and living happily ever after.

**MY LIFE LESSON &
QUOTES TO LIVE BY**

- *Put God first in every aspect of your life.*

- *Take accountability.*

- *Never settle.*

- *When people show you who they are, believe them*

- *If you are not being treated like a king or queen, then leave, there will be someone who will treat you the way you deserve.*

- *Love yourself first before you love anyone else.*

- *You are worth being loved the right way.*

- Have confidence.

37

Jaivon's
World

"EVERY DAY I FEEL IS A BLESSING FROM GOD. AND I CONSIDER IT A NEW BEGINNING. YEAH EVERYTHING IS BEAUTIFUL."

-Prince

It was coming closer to my due date, and I was getting bigger each day. I was all belly, as they say. I weighed 114 pounds before I was pregnant. After, I weighed 130 pounds and had chicken legs and arms. I was overdue, so my older brother and I decided to walk in hopes that my water would break. I walked from my home for two miles, to the store and back—still nothing. My brother and I decided to take a drive to see my cousin on the South Side of Chicago. My cousin was so happy to see me and was in disbelief that I had gotten so big. We were talking in back of the house and reminiscing and having a good time, but my bladder was so weak, and I needed to use the bathroom. I went into this house to use the bathroom and came back to exchange hugs and say bye. Who would have known that this would be the last time that I would see my cousin alive, and that a year later, her son would transition. Life is too short; we need to love each other, because we don't know when it will be our last day. After that long day of walking and riding, I was exhausted and went to sleep.

While waiting for the baby to make his entrance, I received a phone call from an old friend, Steven, whom I had thought I would never hear from again. I had not talked to him in over a year, so this was an extreme surprise. He was a sweet person and cared about me deeply. I was young and had made certain decisions that I regret, but I was happy to hear from him. We talked for almost an hour, laughing and joking, but I knew I had to tell him about my pregnancy. My voice became low and shaky. "Steven, I want to tell you something." In a low pitch, he said, "Yeah."

"I am pregnant." The phone was now silent for what felt like an eternity. I said, "Hello?" He stated, "I'm here— just in shock." I stated, "Would you still be my friend?" He stated, "Yes!" A sigh of relief took over my body, knowing that he knew. After that conversation we decided it was time to get off the phone. Although Steven was in another state, we would keep in contact. It was time for me to focus on having this baby. I was scared and nervous.

The baby was due October 31, 2007, but he refused to come on that date. I can't blame him for not wanting to come into this crazy world. The time was getting closer for me to deliver. I was nervous and scared and didn't know what to expect. I was told by the nurse to come to the hospital on November 8, 2007, to have my labor induced. I could not eat anything but ice chips all day. I arrived at the hospital at 3:15 p.m. By 7:00 a.m. I was miserable. I could not eat; the baby was stubborn and did want to come. Ugh. I was given an epidural to help with the pain. I sat up while the doctor stuck a large needle in my spine, ensuring that I did not move an inch. I was so nervous and was told that if I moved, I would be paralyzed. I was in so much pain and tired of anticipating what would come next.

Then, boom, that pain kicked in. It felt like I was being punched in the stomach multiple times, and at that point, I knew it was time. This was nothing like TV. I thought the baby was supposed to just pop out, but no, I was in excruciating pain. I yelled and screamed, "Get this baby out of me." It felt like one of those movies where an alien had invaded my body and was trying to come out. In the midst of the pain, I released a bowel movement as I pushed and pushed. Charlie was in the room with me; I could see his face as he looked in disgust. He sat there patiently waiting the arrival of our new addition. Finally, on November 9, 2007, at 8:27 a.m., I had a healthy baby boy weighing eight pounds, six ounces and measuring twenty-one inches. Welcome to the world, Jaivon Centrell. As I looked at him, he was so precious. I held him for a moment after he was cleaned. I was exhausted. I was ripped from my vaginal area to my buttocks. I was wondering how people could have multiple children. I couldn't believe that rip was from only one baby.

One thing about me is that I love pictures and capturing moments. I had to make sure my son was fly for his pictures. He wore a royal blue Nike hat and the jumpsuit to match. He reminded me of my baby photos. He was my twin but a boy version. I was so happy.

I received a free car seat through a program for low- income families at Cook County Hospital. I was so grateful and thankful. Charlie set up the car seat and picked us up from the hospital. He wanted me to stay with him at his mother's home, but I wanted to stay with my mom. I felt more comfortable being at my mother's home. Plus, his mother's house was an hour away. I was not healed and was bleeding frequently. I was in so much pain and wanted to ensure that I was able to take Jaivon to his doctor's appointment. At that time, I was so frustrated and didn't know how to be a parent. I did not have any little nieces or nephews at the time, so I was unaware of how to take care of a child. Sandra would often come over to help with the baby. I was learning how to feed, clean, and nurture him. I even had a chart to keep a log of when I was supposed to feed the baby according to the information that I read about how to take care of a baby after pregnancy. I later realized that this schedule was not feasible, and I started feeding the baby differently. I realized that a baby is usually crying for a couple of reasons: they're hungry, they're wet, or they want attention. I was a little late, but I eventually picked up the cues. I even purchased a CD called "Baby Body Moving" to help me soothe him. Like I said, I was figuring it out. It was Jaivon's world, and it was no longer just about me. Thank God I had my parents to assist me with this new adventure, because I don't know how I would have gotten through being a new parent without them.

Charlie's mother stopped by to see the baby and drop off the gift for the baby shower. We chatted for a moment, and then she left. She was an active member of the church and would attend various functions and was extremely busy, but she always made time for her grandchildren. I was thankful that she was able to see him for the first time. Charlie would come over; he loved both of his sons. He would often have Jaivon on his chest, and they would both fall asleep. I took a picture I thought was so adorable. I was happy that I had the family I always wanted. I felt like my life was complete.

Charlie took me to multiple doctor appointments, but at times, he was not that engaged I had to take Jaivon to the doctor, and I was in extreme pain. While at the doctor's office, I was struggling with the car seat and the baby, and he left me there alone. He later came back to pick us up, but I felt like he could have stayed and helped more. Looking back I see that I experienced multiple forms of abuse. I was young, and this was my first love, so I ignored multiple signs. To be honest, I didn't even know what the signs were, and I thought some of the behavior was normal. Charlie and I had our ups and downs, but we were working through our rough patches. Charlie would sometimes embarrass me in front of his family by cursing me out or making a statement about how I couldn't do anything right, which was uncalled for. I would talk back to him, but it would always be an argument. I would stand up for myself and was not a pushover, but it was something about him I just couldn't shake. I felt like I was under his spell at times. Sometimes I hated it, and other times I loved it. I knew he loved me even though we went through a lot. Every relationship goes through difficulties, right? But it is sticking it out that really matters.

Charlie and I both lived with our parents, so it was difficult for us to have that family dynamic of living together. I knew that we could not continue to live in separate locations. I felt like if we were grown enough to have a baby, then we should be able to venture out on our own and take care of our responsibilities. We were on good terms at this point and decided to start searching for a home. We were young, so many people did not want to take the chance to rent to us. We were able to find an apartment in the western suburbs that was not that far from Chicago. That was perfect; my job was within walking distance, and it still allowed me to travel to see family and friends. I was working in the banking industry, and Charlie was working in the restaurant industry, which allowed us to afford a two- bedroom apartment. I thought we had finally arrived. At that time, I felt like life was all about perception. I was a beautiful twenty-two-year-old woman who had a banking job, lived in the western suburbs, and drove a decent car. Charlie had just purchased a new Lincoln LX that I could stunt in. We were working together and purchasing brand-new furniture—a new queen-size bedroom set for our room as well as one for our son. I felt like we were building something. The first year was great! Charlie's older son would visit; we were the perfect blended family. I looked at his son as if he were my own. I had never had any problems with the other mother of his child. There was no drama on my end or hers. Charlie and I would have family night and would rent Redbox movies and order pizza. We would cuddle and bond. We enjoyed creating memories with our family.

We were together all the time and began to argue frequently, but that was expected with any relationship, right? Charlie could be a little controlling at times and did not want me going out. I still went outside but had to deal with the arguments when I came back in. It seemed like the arguments were becoming constant, and it was drawing us further away from each other. I felt like I was advancing in different areas in my life. I was excelling at my job and went back to school. I felt that Charlie feared I would leave him if I continued to grow and pursue my dreams.

I was in school in pursuit of my associate's degree in art. I slowed down a little after having my son. Prior to having him, I was working two jobs, going to school, and purchasing my first vehicle. I slowed down and only worked one job—well, two— because being a mom is a job in itself. I was a full-time mom, worked full time, and went to school part time. I was extremely immersed in learning new things and loved school. After taking a year off, I was ready to start back and fulfill my goal of graduating. I was hard on myself with everything. Although I had a lot going on and was doing so much, I felt like a failure. It was three years, and I was still in junior college. It was only supposed to take two years. My younger brother had graduated with his bachelor's degree, and I was still here without any degree. I was seeing fresh faces in the school. Time was passing me by right before my eyes. Most of my friends or associates had already graduated or dropped out, but here I was, still there. I was so stressed, dealing with things at home and school and work. It was difficult, but I was determined to continue to make a better life for my son. As I continued to pursue my dreams, it seemed like Charlie and I were going in different directions.

We were now in our home for the second year, and it seemed like things were gradually falling apart. The arguments were becoming more intense. It was to the point that I did not want to go home. I had a smart mouth, but I was feeling drained and tired of the frequent arguments. I tried to work my problems away, and I even stayed at school longer hours to get away from the chaos. Charlie could be the sweetest person, but don't get him upset. He would go off. I tried to keep him happy, but I felt like I was walking on eggshells. I wanted to make him happy and not be angry. I even tried to ignore him at times to prevent arguments. There was a time I was trying to ignore Charlie and was texting on my phone. He decided to snatch my phone and break it. There went another argument between us that was toxic, but it could be good at times too. He purchased a new phone for me the next day. Still, I was like, why would you do that? I was growing extremely tired of the pattern and often confided in my friend Steven. We had a great connection, and he would provide me with advice. I appreciated him for being an ear to listen. He would send Jaivon gifts, which I would always state that I could not accept. But he would not take no for an answer. I would often wish that Steven was the father of my child so that maybe I wouldn't be going through this. He was there for me and accepted my son. That meant a lot. Talking to Steven was an outlet from Charlie, and it made me feel good to talk to someone who didn't judge me. He was there for me and my son. He was really appreciated during this time, because I don't know what I would have done. I also talked to Steven's mom, who referred to my son as her grandson. I hoped she was aware that this was not Steven's baby, but Charlie's. She did not care. I had a great relationship with her.

My relationship with Charlie's mom felt awkward, and I often wondered what I could do to make us become closer. I did not know what it was about me, but I felt like she didn't like me, and that kept our relationship at a distance. I guess I will never know.

Love Will Make You Put Up With Some Crazy Things

"I AM NOT WHAT HAPPENED TO ME.
I AM WHAT I CHOOSE TO BECOME."

-Carl Jung

At this point Charlie decided he was not paying rent any more. He would often make up excuses, saying there was something wrong with his debit card or that he had lost it and that his check would come soon. This was placing me further in debt and making it difficult to stay afloat. I decided to work extra hard at work, gaining bonuses every two weeks. That was not enough, so I decided to take out payday loans to cover the rent and other bills. It also helped me take care of Jaivon. The payday loans only helped so much, though. Soon I found myself right back at the beginning, with no money. I took out five different payday loans to play catch-up on my bills, but the interest was making it hard for me to get out of debt. Charlie was not helping me with anything; he would barely take groceries in the house. I know what you are thinking: "I would have kicked him out. Why were you putting up with that?" Legally, we had a joint lease, meaning he had the same rights as me, and I could not kick him out. Charlie had even informed me that the mother of his older son had placed him on child support for both of her kids. She had just recently had a daughter who was two months old. I thought about it but dismissed the idea. I was just getting tired. I don't know what that situation was about, and I never investigated it. All I did know was that I was tired.

I just continued to deal with the situation, hoping things would get better. I would complain, and he would try to do some things like take out the trash or pay a phone bill, but it was not enough. I was extremely miserable, but I still loved Charlie. It's kind of hard to explain, as I stated earlier, but he had a special hold on me. I would get off work and have severe migraines. My hair was falling out, and I was stressed. I guess that is what stress can do to you. People said, "She will leave when she's had enough"—I was at that point. I barely had money to buy the things I wanted for my son and me. From the outside it looked perfect, but from the inside, it was chaos and dysfunction. I tried my best to make the relationship work and did not want to be a single parent, but it looked like it was getting to that point. I was carrying the most weight, and it was destroying me mentally, physically, emotionally, and spiritually. I did not know how much longer I could put up with it. I prayed every day to God and expressed my frustrations and asked him to take me out of this chaos. I felt like I was on a downward spiral and did not know what to do. I kept my faith, but I wanted to be out of this relationship. And I was tired of being drained and wanted to be happy again. I felt like I did not have anyone to talk to about everything and tried to handle it all myself. I guess you could have called me Super Malina, but I was not. I was too embarrassed to tell my family. I continued to channel my frustrations into my work and education, hoping that I would not be in this position forever. I was tired of trying to look like I had everything together. Instead, I was struggling.

I was busy going to school and working all the time. My mother would have to babysit my son almost every day. I would usually have Jaivon on the days that I did not have to attend school and have mother-and-son time. I felt bad that I could not be a stay-at-home mom, to have an even closer relationship with my son. I felt like I was abandoning him because I was working full time and going to school part time to create a better future for him.

I wanted to make sure that I was aware of the

things that my son enjoyed. His favorite cartoon character at the time was SpongeBob SquarePants, but as he got older, he was fascinated with Iron Man. It felt so good to finally spend time with him. We enjoyed going to the park, eating pizza and ice cream, and finishing the night watching SpongeBob together. I loved to live and cherish the moments, but I didn't know where this little boy got it from. He loved to take pictures. I guess he came by it honestly because I would always take pictures. He would always have a big, bright smile on his face like his mother. I would always say that our smiles could light up the room.

I felt like sometimes it was hard to smile because of my financial situation. I did not have a lot of money because I was paying all the bills, and it was difficult to pay for events to entertain my son. I would find ways that were less expensive to entertain him and took frequent trips to the park and library. It was cost-efficient, and it allowed us to spend time together. He loved movies, so I let him pick out different videos that we could watch. I would pick out videos that were educational and would help with learning how to speak better. Jaivon had trouble speaking and would often point at items instead of pronouncing the words. Jaivon was two years old, and I felt like he should be speaking more words and forming sentences. I was concerned, and I had to do some research to find a speech therapist in the area. I was reading somewhere where it stated that, around that age, learning and speaking were critical in the growth of a child's development. I still had my medical benefits through public aid, but a lot of places did not accept this insurance. I contacted the medical benefits department and was able to arrange for a speech therapist to come out to my home. I was feeling relieved. I also had to take Jaivon to the hospital for a hearing test and provide the results to the therapist. The results of his hearing came back that everything was fine. The only thing that he really needed help with was his speaking. The therapist began coming twice a week, and after two months, he was progressing and learning how to form sentences. I was so excited to see that this service was working for him.

It seemed like things were falling into place, and after five years of being a student at Wilbur Wright Community College, I finally graduated. I know that junior college is usually two years, but it took me five years because I had been going through a lot. I realized that, through all my struggles, it had paid off. I finally had the degree that I had been working so hard for. I understood that it was not how long it took, but that, essentially, I was able to accomplish my goal. I decided to enroll at Northeastern Illinois University to obtain my bachelor's degree. I was eager to start this new journey for Jaivon and me. I just wanted him to have a better life.

I had one part of my life going right and was excited, but my romantic life with Charlie was ending. I could not take it anymore and decided that since the lease was almost up at our apartment complex, I would have to put my pride aside and reach out to my family.

Charlie wanted me to come live with him and his family, but I decided that I should go and stay with my family for a short period until I had things sorted out. While I was making my decisions, Charlie decided to move everything out of the apartment along with all our clothing. I went back and stayed with my family, but I did not have anything. I had the few clothes that I had left behind before I had moved out, but that was it. Charlie took everything and put it in his mother's garage. I did not want to see him, because I knew he would try to make me stay at her house, so I decided to stay away. I know that it was hard to be away from Charlie, but for the first time in years, I felt free!

The winters in Chicago are not a joke, and this one was brutal. It was extremely cold, but I felt relieved by being away from Charlie. I would call his mother almost every day to see if I could come get the clothing for me and my son. She would reply, "Wait until he goes to work." I would wait, but Charlie had decided to stop working. I knew he was dealing with several deaths in his family and was grieving, but it seemed like Charlie was dealing with depression and was not getting the help that he needed. This breakup was a difficult part of my life.

I Love You,

But

I Love Me More,

" I MUST UNDERTAKE TO LOVE MYSELF
AND TO RESPECT MYSELF AS THOUGH
MY VERY LIFE DEPENDS UPON
SELF-LOVE AND SELF-RESPECT."

-Maya Angelou

I know that Charlie took everything, but I told him to keep both of his cars, because I did not want any ties to him. I wanted to be free and start fresh. I missed Charlie, and my heart was hurting, because I loved him with all of me. I think I loved him more than I loved myself and needed this time to find myself again. I had lost myself within this relationship and needed time to discover who I was as a person and what made me happy.

Charlie started popping up at my job trying to apologize, but I did not want to hear it. I was glad that one of my coworkers would pick me up for work, but I would try to avoid Charlie at all costs and would take a different route when I was going home. I would get on a different bus so that he would not see me. Charlie even came inside of my workplace begging on his knees for me to take him back. I stated, "This is my place of employment. Don't bring this to my job." It went from him popping up at my job almost every day to frequent phone calls. He called so often that I had to disconnect my home phone and cut my cell phone off to get peace. This went on for roughly two months and then the calls began to subside. Eventually there were not any calls from Charlie. We had been together for five years, and it was extremely hard to let him go, but I felt that this would be best for the both of us. As I stated earlier, I wanted to be free, and I finally felt like I was obtaining that freedom. It was difficult, but it felt so good not having arguments every day. I could finally breathe and not feel like I was walking on eggshells.

I still had to make sure my son and I had some type of finances coming in. I had to take money from my 401(k) as a hardship to ensure that my son and I had the essentials. It was not much but would help until I got another paycheck. I was extremely busy. Let me provide a rundown of my typical day. I would wake up at 3:00 a.m. and take two buses and a train to be at work by 7:00 a.m. I worked until 3:00p.m. Once I got off work, I would take the bus to NEIU and attend class from 6:00 p.m. to 9:00 p.m. I would then catch the bus to make it home and would usually make it there around 10:00 p.m. I would then iron Jaivon's clothing to ensure that he had something to wear, since I had recently enrolled him in school. I would have to continue this process until I was able to obtain a car to reduce the travel time. I was waiting for my income tax refund to get a car, and hopefully, I could get more rest, because I was exhausted. But I knew everything would pay off later.

I was excited about Jaivon's enrollment into the nearby learning center that would help him improve his social skills and progress in his speech. I signed him up for their transportation service. My mom and Jaivon would travel together on the learning center's bus to the school. I was extremely overprotective, so I asked my mom if she would ride with him. I wanted to ensure that he made it to school safely every day. It added to my expenses for sure. I would have to come up with $300 every two weeks, but I had to do what I needed to do to ensure that he had the best. It was difficult, but God was able to help me through this rough time.

It had been five months since I had heard from Charlie. Our son would always ask about his dad and his nana, who was Charlie's mother. Jaivon loved her. She was always active in her grandchildren's lives, but during this time, she was not active due to the rough patch with Charlie and me. I hoped that this would blow over and he could go back to visit her.

It was now December, and I did not have much money, but I wanted Jaivon to have a great Christmas. I purchased $150 worth of toys at Dollar General. It was the best I could do during that time. He was so excited, and it felt good to see that big, bright smile. It made my day. He had the guitar that I purchased and was singing his heart out in his new Iron Man underwear. He even renamed himself Jaivon Iron Man. I was disappointed that Charlie did not call or even provide anything for our son. I felt like I was getting into a better place in my life. I was regaining my independence. It was Jaivon and I starting over together.

MY LIFE LESSON & QUOTES TO LIVE BY

- *Never give up on your dreams, no matter how long it takes.*

- *Don't let life break you. Instead, learn from it and become a better version of you.*

- *You are the narrator of your life*

- *Hard times won't last always. Keep going; God's got you.*

- *Do the best you can. You will never be perfect.*

- *Cherish every moment in life.*

Pain& Suffering

"THERE IS NO TIMESTAMP ON TRAUMA. THERE ISN'T A FORMULA THAT YOU CAN INSERT YOURSELF INTO TO GET FROM HORROR TO HEALED. BE PATIENT. TAKE UP SPACE. LET YOUR JOURNEY BE THE BALM."

-Dawn Serra

It had been months, and still there was no communication with Charlie. I became used to it. I was still struggling financially because of all the loans that I had taken out previously to maintain the household before I left, and now I had new expenses such as the $300 transportation service, school, and other bills. I had at least five or six loans out, plus interest was being added. My father was helping me pay down some of them. I was strained, but God continued to get me through, and I was making it. I knew that I was struggling, but in the midst of my struggle, I felt like I was moving forward. In that moment I was happy again and knew that everything was coming together. Jaivon was in school, his speech was getting better, and I was working and in school. It was finally income tax time, and I was able to purchase a car for transportation.

It was now spring, and the holidays were out of the way. I decided to stop by my sister's house to catch up. I sat on her bed with my phone in my back pocket, and it must have dialed someone. I could hear the person saying, "Hello. Hello." I removed the phone from my back pocket and answered it. To my surprise it was Charlie. We talked for a brief moment. He stated several times that "he missed his family, he wanted to see his son," and "blah, blah"—you know the rest. I was happy to hear from him but was conflicted because of how he had treated me in the past. A couple of days went by, so I decided to let Charlie see his son despite my personal feelings. Our son was overjoyed to see his father and really missed him. Charlie wanted to take him to the park and buy Jaivon some new clothes. That was fine with me, and I appreciated Charlie buying him clothes and shoes, but he still needed food and essentials, not to mention money for his new school and the transportation service. I needed real help from his father. I hate it when a person thinks they've really contributed by buying one thing, but they've been missing in action and nowhere to be found when the going got tough. They have completely been out of the picture. It was the two of us, Charlie and I, who had a baby, but only one of us was taking care of our child, me. Charlie was unemployed, so he didn't have much money. I only asked if he could pick Jaivon up and drop him off at the learning center; that would have helped tremendously. It would cut the transportation cost, and I could buy more food and pay down some of the loans. Charlie decided to pick up Jaivon from school. I felt like things might work. He would continuously state that he wanted his family back, but I continued to decline his offer. I had this tough exterior, but I wished our family could have been together the right way. I had made my decision, and I was enjoying my newfound freedom.

My birthday was coming up, and I wanted to look super cute. It was my twenty-fifth birthday, so you know I had to do it big. I decided to save some money to get my hair done and purchase my outfit, shoes, manicure, pedicure, etc. I went to the beauty shop and had this pretty curly hair to match my brown, round face. I loved my hair, and I was feeling myself again. I thought I looked beautiful. I really wanted to go somewhere to show off my new look.

Charlie wanted to go to the store and get Jaivon a couple of things for school, so I decided to join him. We were leaving the store, and that is when we got into an argument while Jaivon was in the back seat of the car. Charlie pulled out my weave that had just been installed by the stylist for my birthday. I could not believe that he had ruined my hair for my birthday. I was so embarrassed and hated that my son saw this type of behavior. It was a good thing I had more hair in the house. I went back to the shop with a ponytail in my hair. I was so embarrassed. My stylist was confused, because I had just left with my hair done, but now it looked a mess. I explained what had happened and was hoping that he would do my hair without me paying another fee. I could see in my stylist's eyes that he felt sorry for me and decided to do my hair for my birthday without any charge. I was so embarrassed and kept this type of abuse to myself. I told Charlie to leave and that I did not want to see him again. My son cried for his father, but I thought this was for the best.

The day finally came. It was my birthday, and I decided to go to a club. Charlie called earlier to wish me a happy birthday, but I was not trying to hear that. I was trying to have a good birthday. About ten of us went out that night, and a couple of my other friends could not get in, because it was filled. Everyone came out to celebrate with me—my brother, cousins, friends, and, of course, me. I got multiple gifts. My brother bought rounds of liquor for everyone, and I kept putting drinks back. I was dancing and enjoying myself. I realize that we must enjoy each moment in life, because we never know when things will change. It was a great night. I think I had one too many, but my friends made sure I made it home safely. My birthday was out of the way, and it was time to get back to reality.

Charlie continued to apologize for his behavior. He said that he was homeless and sleeping on benches because he had gotten into an argument with his mother and some of his family members. In my mind I did not want him to be homeless, so once again, I put my personal feelings aside. I know it sounds stupid. I asked my mom if Charlie could stay in the back bedroom that was vacant, and I would stay in the front bedroom. Charlie agreed to take Jaivon to school again to help out, and I agreed. He made a pallet on the bedroom floor in the back of the apartment. I was completely fine with coparenting, but that was it. I was done trying to have a romantic relationship with him. I had tried in the past, but I did not want to be with him anymore. I could tell that the romantic relationship had taken a toll on me. My self-esteem had been extremely low, to the point that I did not think I was beautiful anymore. The previous time away from Charlie had made me realize that I deserved so much better. I was finally regaining my confidence and becoming conscious of the beautiful queen that I was.

Life was good for me. I finished my first semester at NEIU in the social work department with all As. I finally realized what I wanted to do in my career; this profession just meshed well with me.

I was eager to sign up for the next semester. I was feeling good. The sun was shining, and I knew it was going to be a good day. I woke up and decided to enroll in my second semester at NEIU. I was about to leave when Charlie asked if he could go with me, so Jaivon, Charlie, and I went to the school. I completed registration. I was so excited about this new journey in my life. Charlie seemed agitated, and he yelled at Jaivon to stop tapping on the window. I told Charlie not to yell at him, which later escalated into an argument.

Looking back now, I feel like he may have been jealous of my accomplishments and my willingness to continue to move and strive for more in my life. We returned to the house. I noticed my parents still had not arrived home. We were in the house when my best friend called and stated she had tickets to this new fitness pole dancing class. Since she was one of the people that was unable to get into the club that night, she decided to surprise me with the class. I was gathering my workout gear in the bedroom when

Charlie asked me where I was going. I got smart and said, "It is none of your business." He walked out of the room. He came back within a minute and closed the door and pushed me on the bed. He began to unzip his pants and pull my shorts off. I was fighting to stop Charlie. I grabbed his penis to prevent it from being inserted into my vagina, but he overpowered me and released himself into me. At that moment I felt helpless; he then stabbed me in my left side toward my neck. The next stab was in my arm. I was terrified and in disbelief. He was not on top of me anymore but was more focused on stabbing me at this point. I got up and ran for the door and felt another slash across my neck with this large butcher knife. Struggling, we both fell, and he now pierced my breast, trying to stab me in the heart. All I could think about at that moment was, is this how I die? My life was flashing before my eyes. I somehow grabbed the knife that was piercing me through my breast and ran to the door but was unable to get out because of the multiple locks. I ran to the window and threw the knife out of the window. I could still remember Charlie's eerie voice saying, "What you do that for?" I was losing blood, and I was in the window yelling for help. I was halfway in and halfway out of a window of a tall two-flat building. I knew that if I fell, I could be hurt, and was scared since there was nothing but concrete below. Charlie began to punch me in the face, pushing me out the window. I could see people looking at the commotion. There was also a funeral at the church. I remember looking out the window earlier that day. I fell onto the concrete and was able to get up and run for help. It had to be angels looking over me. I always say that my uncle was helping me. He had died three months earlier. Also, God was helping me in this situation. I felt something in my spirit that was saying, "Something is not right with Jaivon." I was looking for help for my son as I was losing blood and becoming lightheaded. I went to a white security car in the middle of the busy street. I did not have any shorts or underwear on, because he had ripped them off when he raped me. My shirt was torn, and blood was all over. I saw a police van and ran to it to get help for my son and me.

The officer went to the door, which was steel and automatically locked without a key. The neighbors came and let him in as I stood across the street helpless and bloody, feeling like I was about to faint. People just surrounded me in disbelief, waiting on the ambulance to come to the scene. It seems like if you live in the hood, it takes longer to get assistance, although the hospital was not that far away. Finally, the ambulance arrived. I asked where my son was. "Where is my son? I need my son." At that moment something did not feel right; no one was answering. My mom arrived, and my neighbor let her know that I was in the ambulance. I could see the worry on her face as they closed the ambulance doors and drove off.

I arrived at the county hospital and was taken into the trauma unit. I kept asking, "Where is Jaivon? Where is Jaivon?" I kept replaying our last conversation. No one was answering me. I could see the expression on the officer's face. She did not have to say anything. I knew Jaivon was gone. I was questioned by the police, but I wanted to know where my son was. I didn't care about anything else, not even my own life. The news spread like wildfire. I am a semiprivate person, but now it was on the news. It was everywhere. I remember telling Charlie's mom what he had done. His family and mine were at the hospital. After hours of being in the hospital, my family told me that Jaivon was dead. My heart sank into my chest. "What? How could this be? I was just with my baby." The pain was unbearable as I was wheeled into the room to see him. The white sheet covered his neck. I could see blood in that area. I held his lifeless hand and saw cuts on his tiny arms. My heart hurt, and no one could do anything to help me. I felt lost and in disbelief and knew my life would never be the same.

I did not want to go back to the house where the events took place. I was too traumatized. How could a father do something like that? It was one thing to do something to me, but to our child who had nothing to do with our disagreement? Jaivon was three and a half, and we were planning for his fourth birthday party. He'd said, "I want an Iron Man birthday party." Now instead, I was planning his funeral. Why was this happening to me? I did not deserve this. All I had tried to do was help people. I had just wanted to help Charlie. Why would he have done this? These questions took over my head.

I decided to stay at my uncle's house, where my family was a strong presence during this time. My mom, dad, brothers, uncles, aunts, and so many cousins were there. I had cousins from all over checking on me and making sure I was okay. The night I came to my uncle's house, I went into the bathroom and saw a knife and thought to myself, I might as well finish it. My son was my life, and I did not know how I would carry on and wanted to die without him. That is how much I loved my son. My life was flipped upside down. I went to sleep that night holding his favorite Iron Man book bag that he'd once held when he went to school. I smelled the book bag for his scent. My son, my baby, was gone. Words cannot describe this feeling. It felt so cold in the room. I asked for covers and had at least three on but was still cold. I felt like that was my son lying near me. I felt like I was a failure. The one job I had had on earth was to protect my child, and I couldn't do that. I had thought I was making the right choice to allow a father to be a part of his child's life. I did not want to be a bitter person. What I felt was the right thing ultimately was the wrong thing, and now my son was not here. I felt so hurt.

The next day arrived. I did not want to eat or dress, but the police came early that morning. My family was all there, and the police requested to speak to me alone. My older brother refused to leave me. I was asked why I had let Charlie babysit. I said, "I thought he could be—" But before I got the words out of my mouth, my brother said, "How can you babysit your own child?" Charlie was telling the police that I had pushed our son on him, which was not the case. I went to the police station where I was interrogated like I had done something wrong. I felt so confused as to why I was being questioned like this when I was the victim and a grieving mother. I was being treated like a criminal. I was extremely exhausted, and in my mind, I was terrified that Charlie would find me and kill me. I cried day and night. No one could help me with this pain. I did not want to eat. I just wanted to be out of this nightmare. Can you imagine having everyone from all over knowing what happened? I was a private person and did not want people to know what was going on in my life. It was all over the news and in the newspapers. It was a horrible time in my life; I was so disgusted. I just wanted to hide and not face this. The only way to describe it is to say that my heart hurt. It was an uncontrollable heartache that would never go away. Not only was my business being put out for the world to see, but also I was being criticized by people that didn't even know me. I had certain family members siding with him, but I felt like right is right and wrong is wrong—no matter who you are.

After the exhausting day at the police department, I went to sleep and woke up to another day of sadness. Someone from the Department of Children and Family Services (DCFS) introduced herself as Christina. She looked like a blow-up doll with big breasts. She wanted to ask questions. I had told the events to multiple people and was just drained in addition to not having been able to sleep. It was all taking a toll on my body. I passed her the newspaper article and stated, "Read this. That's what happened." I was wondering why she was here. My son was deceased. After our encounter I walked her to the door, where she stated, "You need to pick better men in the future." I was weak and just was taken aback by her comment. How was I supposed to know that this man would do this? Why was I getting blamed for everything? Who was she to say that to me? I had just lost my son and had to plan for his funeral, and that was what she said? I was so angry. I contacted her supervisor, but he stated it was her word against mine, since no one else was around to verify it. She later called and provided an apology that was not sincere at all.

I did not want to do anything. My family had to help me with everything. As I stated before, family came from all over to see me. My cousin who is a nurse would come over to change my wound dressings to make sure they didn't get infected. My mom and aunt would put clothes on me— things I would never wear—but I didn't care. I would not comb my hair. I was depressed. I was lost. My life was turned upside down.

The day I dreaded was coming closer: my son's funeral. I went to get my hair done the day before, and my aunt took me to find something to wear. I woke up with an emptiness in my heart, but knew I had to face this day head on. I got dressed and got in the limousine to go to church. Thank God for my family, especially my brothers. They really helped me by planning everything; my strength was gone. Charlie's uncle allowed the funeral to be at his church, which was awkward, but I was not thinking clearly. When I went into the church, it was one side of his family and the other side my family. It was a big church, and I was surprised war didn't break out. When people would come to give the family a hug, I noticed some of his family would just walk past, not acknowledging me at all. How disrespectful was that? But all I could think about was that my son was in that casket. Charlie's mother dressed in white as if she were going to a wedding and stated that she wanted to match what my son had on. It was extremely awkward, and she had dressed Jaivon's older brother in the same suit as my son. My brother spoke some words, and my uncle sang at the funeral. To tell the truth, I felt like my son was a part of the family to a certain extent. Charlie's uncle began to preach but didn't focus much on Jaivon's life. Instead, he tried to convince others of how his sister was a good mother. I was thinking, What the hell does this have to do with my son? I kept staring at the casket, blocking out any words anyone was saying. After the service came to an end, everyone left, and I went to say goodbye to my son. I rubbed his chest, feeling how hard it was, and was looking at the bruise they had attempted to cover up on his light-skinned face. I continued to stare and rub him. "My baby, my baby," was all I could say. The ushers came over and told me it was time to go, but I couldn't leave him. They had to pick me up and carry me away kicking and screaming. My family had to help me calm down and get ready for the burial.

I went to the burial site and released balloons in his honor with pain and sorrow. As I went back to the car, I could hear an argument breaking out. There were two separate repasts, but my family did not want anything to do with any of his family. I attended both of them. I wanted to keep the peace, but it was too late—Charlie had changed everything. I stayed for a short time with Charlie's family and later went where all my family was. It was difficult going back into that building where Jaivon had been murdered and where I had been raped and stabbed. It was traumatizing, but I went to tell my family I appreciated them for being there for me. I was unaware of some people who were my cousins, but I appreciated them being there during this tough time in my life.

The burial of my son was the most painful thing I have ever faced. My heart still hurts today. My ultimate goal was to be a great parent. To be completely honest, I feel like I failed as a parent and was not able to fulfill that goal. His life was cut short, and I will not be able to see him get older. What I was experiencing was enough to have made me start drinking or doing drugs. Not only was my everyday life being examined, but it was being played out on social media, in the news, and in other media outlets. I remember looking on Facebook at all the comments under the article. One stated, "She was uneducated and looking for any man she could get." I was in disbelief at some of the comments. I saw one from a familiar person, Charlie's cousin. The comment read, "FREE CHARLIE." I could not believe what I was reading. He just murdered his child, and you want to free him? As time progressed, this provided me some insight on some of Charlie's family's perspective. I knew that I could not be consumed by this negativity. It felt like I was stuck inside a ball of chaos, confusion, and all-around negativity.

I was in disarray, wondering what I would do with my life now. It looked completely different not having Jaivon there. Anyone who has lost someone they love knows that it is hard to get your life back on track, especially from a tragedy. I did not know how and what my next steps in life would be. I knew that I wanted justice for my son. My life would never be the same, and I knew that. I did know that I wanted to help others, so they would not have to feel the way I had or have to deal with what I was going through. I felt like God had kept me here for a reason; I just didn't know what it was yet. I continued to pray and believe in God about the next ventures in my life.

After The Pain

"I CAN BE CHANGED BY WHAT HAPPENS TO ME, BUT I REFUSE TO BE REDUCED BY IT."

-Maya Angelou

After going through this trauma, it was taking a toll on me physically, mentally, and emotionally. I could not sleep at all. I felt like a zombie. I would go without sleeping for days. I would take naps throughout the day, but that would be for two hours at the most. I was not eating. I was forced to eat crackers to keep from getting sick. I had so many emotions and was in fear for my life. In my mind, I thought he would try to come back to kill me.

I was still a customer service representative at a bank, but I was on a leave of absence; I could not work in the state I was in. I needed to grieve my son's death and was working on piecing my life together. I did not want to talk, and I continued to pray to God about my problems. The only way to describe it is feeling like an alien all alone on another planet where no one understood me. As much as my family wanted to help, they could not feel the pain that I was going through. It was my journey, and I had to travel this alone. It was me and God—that was it. I had to rely and depend on him.

My family became aware of the signs of my turmoil—my sleeplessness and my absence from the present moment. I would be in a daze, staring for a long time in mid-conversation. I was paranoid, thinking that he was still going to kill me, although he was locked away. I was scared to go anywhere by myself. I could not believe this was my life— living in fear.

My family decided that they had done all they could do, but I needed professional help. My family wanted me to go to therapy. There was often a stigma that you must be crazy to get mental health services. I did not want to be labeled as crazy or anything in that category. I now know that is untrue, and more people should change their thinking about mental health services.

After days of contemplating what I could lose by going, I agreed to go to therapy. My mom and aunt went with me as I took another step into functioning in this world that was no longer normal. I went to the fourth floor in the elevator as they waited in the lobby. I met with Jasmine, who was around my age, which was twenty-five or twenty-six years old. I thought to myself sarcastically, How is she going to help me? The first session I just sat there not talking much because, I didn't know her or trust her. This went on for five sessions. I was going to therapy, at first, to make my family happy. In one session Jasmine followed up about a conversation that we had in our first session. I could tell that she was listening, so I started to open and have more conversations about the death of my son. I was taking the steps to grieve the death of my son and began working on myself. I felt like a failure and felt deprived of the opportunity to see my son get older. This was a source of pain in my heart that is unexplainable.

We began to work on various goals to help me with the difficulty of guilt, hurt, and sorrow. I also went to a psychiatrist to receive assistance on my journey to recovery. In life things affect each person differently, and people react to pain in unique ways. I wanted to deal with my problems head on instead of taking shortcuts that would ultimately lead me right back to the original problem. It hurt dealing with it, but if I did not, it still would hurt overall. I knew God was getting me through this, because otherwise, I don't know how I would have survived.

While going through the process of getting myself together, I still had to worry about the upcoming court dates. I could not believe that Charlie had pleaded not guilty. It was unbelievable; how could he say he was not guilty when he did this? He took my son, our son, away from me. A real father would have never done this to their child. I continued to attend multiple court dates to hear continuance, continuance, continuance. I just wanted justice to be served for my son so that I could pick up some of the broken pieces of my life. My life would never be complete because Jaivon was not there. I was shattered beyond repair.

I continued to hear people telling me to get over it, but they would never know how it felt unless they went through a pain like this. People kept saying, "It's time to get back to your life," but how could I get back to my life when Jaivon was my life? What did getting back to my life even look like? I was lost and full of hurt and pain, a pain so deep that I would never fully heal. This is a pain that is also felt with losing someone you really love. Your heart will never be the same. You will miss that person forever, but you will learn how to live without them, but it is difficult.

MARGARET JEFFERSON

My Drive:
Northeastern Illinois University

"OUR LIVES BEGIN TO END THE DAY
WE BECOME SILENT ABOUT THINGS
THAT MATTER."

-Martin Luther King

I was starting a new journey while still being in disbelief, broken, all alone, and full of questions about why this was happening to me. I finally made up my mind to reenroll for classes. I had taken a semester off to grieve my son's death, but I knew I wanted to complete school. I had started school to have a better life for my son and wanted to finish that goal. Even though my son was not here physically, I still wanted to receive the education to help someone else. This was an overwhelming time for me in my life, but I knew that God was giving me the strength to keep going.

As I walked back into the doors of NEIU, where Jaivon and I had last walked before he died, it was an emotional moment for me. I was so confused and saddened. My heart dropped with sorrow over all that I had been through. I knew I had to fulfill my purpose by taking these first steps. I walked into the office of the dean of social work and informed her that I wanted to enroll for the next semester. She asked, "How are you doing?" I was trying to be strong and hold back my tears. I said, "Yes, I'm fine." But I began to break down crying right in front of her. I just could not control myself. As I began to stop crying, the dean passed me another tissue and asked me again if I was sure I wanted to enroll for that semester. I looked her in the eyes and said, "Yes." I left the office feeling better, knowing that I was continuing to keep going despite my challenges.

I was completely enrolled for the upcoming semester, eager to learn and accomplish a goal that I had set.

It was my first day of class, and I was shaken and extremely nervous. I did not know what to expect. I was wondering whether I would succeed or if I could handle this. I knew I was determined, but a lot was going on, including the court case. I was focused on my studies and receiving justice for my son. It was another court date, but once again, all I heard was continuance, continuance, continuance. I was so ready for this case to be over. It was extremely frustrating. I continued to wrestle with questions about how he could have done this to his child. How could he have done this to me? I thought he loved me. He knew what he had done. I was tired of going through this. I was overwhelmed but placed all my energy into my studies. In each class I would study more about intimate partner/domestic violence, because I wanted to know more about the topic. My time at NEIU was amazing. I met great people in my cohort who really helped me throughout the program.

It was now my second year, and I remembered walking through those doors and wondering if I would be able to make it in this amount of time. I was proud of myself; I had high grades and a GPA of 3.5, granting me the distinction of cum laude. It seemed like my pain was constructive and fueling my fire to keep attending classes to graduate. I knew that whatever I did, I had to keep going. The dean of social work would always check on me, and she was able to see my growth within that year. She decided to nominate me as the student of the year, and I was asked to speak about resiliency. This was the first time that I had spoken about the death of my son and my resiliency to keep going. When I spoke it felt like a release, like a weight was being lifted off me. It seemed like for the first time I felt free and not ashamed of my past. I hoped that my words would heal and help someone else during my pain and the chaos in my world. I felt like school was my outlet. It felt good to build up the strength to encourage and motivate others.

A couple of weeks later, I was asked to speak at the Homicide Victim Memorial at the State Attorney's Office. I knew that Jaivon would want me to speak for him, so I said yes. The day finally arrived, and I was nervous and did not know if I would be able to speak. As I came into the University of Illinois Chicago (UIC) Forum Auditorium, I could see multiple boards with the faces of people who had been murdered. I continued to go down the long hallway full of faces that had once been filled with life and emotion. It was sad to even think about, but I became emotional after I saw my son's photo on this board. It seemed like I couldn't get myself together. Finally, I was able to control my emotions and began to put all my pain into words. I spoke from my heart, hoping that I would be able to save someone that was going through a difficult time or felt like they wanted to give up on life. I wanted people to understand that even though life is hard, you could get through it. In the Bible Philippians 3:14 says

'I can do all things through Christ that strengthens me.' I have come to realize the reality of Matthew 19:26: 'With God all things are possible.' I am a living testimony. As I looked out into the audience, I saw Officer Scott, the officer who had tried to save my son. I continued to speak and be fearless, knowing that my words would help someone. I was coming to the end of my speech when I saw the entire audience stand up and clap, and I knew there were over one thousand people in attendance. The memorial came to an end, and people began to come to the front of the stage to talk to me about their loved ones. I felt honored and amazed that people shared this information with me. People continued to ask, "How are you so strong?" and all I could say was, "It is God." It was at this moment I knew that my words were making an impact and a difference, and my son would continue to live on. I was rushed off the stage to do a press conference. I felt like that day was the most impactful day of my life.

After the speaking event, I received an email

that stated I had been one of three people nominated by the state attorney's office for Violence Against Women Act (VAWA) Award. I was honored and surprised at the same time. I was doing this to keep Jaivon's memory alive. The day finally came, and I invited my family and friends to support me in this chapter of my life. I was extremely nervous, and my palms were sweating, but I was excited. I was honored to receive this award. This was a big moment for me. I was presented with the award by the state's attorney and mayor; I could not believe it was happening. This was such a memorable moment in my life.

It seemed like my life was coming together but would never be complete without my son. I was still in school during this time and was getting ready to graduate. It was challenging to go to school, prepare for court, and advocate for ending domestic violence. My overall goal was to let people know that my son, Jaivon, was once here and that his life was not in vain. He was a beautiful child and should never be forgotten and will always be in our hearts. It was almost time to graduate when another surprise emerged: I was able to have Jaivon placed into the Domestic Violence Exhibit that traveled the world and would share his story. My son would be seen, and his memory would continue to live on and help others. The goal was to help others and be a blessing while I was on this earth. Jaivon was truly a blessing and continued to display that even though he was not present physically.

The big day had finally come. I was walking across the stage with a picture of Jaivon on a button placed on the right side of my graduation gown. I was overwhelmed by various emotions, but I was happy in a way words just can't explain. I would finally graduate with my bachelor's in social work after five years in junior college and two years at the university. Despite all my pain, God was able to help me get through this; I was filled with gratitude. I had completed what I had set out to do for myself but ultimately for my son. I smiled as I walked across the stage looking at my mom, dad, brothers, nephew, uncles, and aunts watching me. I was overjoyed. I graduated cum laude and was wondering what my next steps would be. Although I had accomplished my long-term goal, I was still miserable, because my son was not physically there to see me graduate. I felt like my happiness was short-lived because I was unable to fulfill my biggest goal, which was to be a mother and watch my son get older. I felt guilty for being happy because my son was not there with me. I suppressed my own happiness; I did not know what it looked or felt like to be happy—I was so numb. It was an exciting and yet emotional time for me, but I finally decided on my next steps in life.

Keep Striving:
Chicago State University

"EDUCATION IS LEARNING WHAT
YOU DIDN'T EVEN KNOW YOU
DIDN'T KNOW."

-Daniel J. Boorstin

I was ready to continue my education and start graduate school. Graduating cum laude had its perks, and I was able to participate in the Advanced Standing Social Work Graduate Program. This would mean that I would be able to obtain my degree in one year, which would be great. The only problem with participating in this program was that it would have to be full time, and I would have to take four classes per semester. I often thought about how far I had come and knew that I could do anything at this point in my life. I was not working, so that was another problem. Where would I get money? How would I be able to make it? I decided to take out a loan big enough for that year. I was a social butterfly to a certain extent, and I was able to meet various people and create friendships. The people I met were a blessing in my life and assisted with my journey. God places some people in our lives to get us to the next level, and they can be a blessing or a lesson.

As the first semester came to an end, I was able to meet more new people in my cohort, and we created a bond. Although I was new in the cohort, the group of people I met inspired me to keep going and study hard. We would meet up on the weekends, creating our study group to encourage and uplift each other. There were many times I wanted to give up, especially with statistics, but we had a group that would help in areas the other person was lacking. The school year came and went so fast.

While at Chicago State University (CSU); I saw a familiar face; it was Sam. We used to work together. He was taking a computer engineering class. It had now been three years since everything had occurred, and I was not going on any dates or even trusting men. That I knew him from my past made it much easier, but I was still apprehensive. We decided to go out to a pizza place. I provided my cousin with his name, license plate number, and phone number. I was so nervous to get back out there, but I wanted to see if there could be something there. Although things did not go anywhere, it was an experience. This was one of many of my dates I would go on in the future that would not go anywhere. I came to realize that domestic violence had not only hurt me physically, but also mentally and emotionally, causing different signs of mental illness and other things that arose from abuse.

Along with trying to start dating and going to school, I was still dealing with court. The state's attorney and advocates were a great assistance to me during this time. Looking back, I see that the team that was assigned to me did a phenomenal job seeking justice for my son. They were extremely hands-on—even my attorney. Ms. S. I really appreciated them all. I started meeting with them frequently to prepare for trial. I tried to do as much as I could not to think about going to court to face this person, I once loved but who had murdered our son and tried to kill me. So many things continued to run through my mind: You already took my life, which was my son, and now you want to drag this out? Why?

It had been a rough semester, and I was moving toward graduation. I channeled my anger and anguish into my studies. I completed my dissertation, which focused on intimate partner abuse among African American teen girls. Everything I had dealt with in my past was placed in this paper, but with statistical data.

I wanted answers. How does this occur? Where does it stem from? I focused on community, family dynamic, religion, and mental health in my writing. I challenged myself, because my overall goal was to help someone else so they wouldn't have to go through what I did. As I stated earlier, I am a blessing and an example that things can happen to you, but God can help you through it. After finishing the dissertation, it was time to get ready for graduation. I had put my blood, sweat, and tears into that paper, but it was also therapeutic for me.

It was finally graduation day. A year had gone by so fast. As I went into the arena for graduation, I placed the button with my son's picture on my gown. I took pictures with family and friends and started to line up to walk across the stage. I was excited and full of joy in my heart, knowing that I accomplished yet another goal. I was next in line, wondering who would cheer for me or if I would trip and fall with these tall heels. As I walked across the stage, I saw Sam and wanted to make sure I did not fall. Thankfully, I made it across the stage and went to my seat. It was a long ceremony. I took pictures and basked in that moment of happiness and placed the date of going to trial in the back of my mind for that day. After going through all this, I encourage people to live and cherish the moments in your life, because you will never get them back—including those with your loved ones. After graduation I went home. The moment of happiness began to fade away. I could not be truly happy, because my son was not there to see yet another accomplishment, and like always, my heart hurt. This is the only way I can describe how I had been feeling; no matter what I did or accomplished, nothing could fill this void or hurt. There was a hole in my heart that would never be filled the way it was when my son was alive. I was still in my twenties, and it seemed like I had been through so much pain, and this was the ultimate pain. Graduation was over now. I had to get back to preparing for court.

Judgement Day

> "WITH FREEDOM COMES
> RESPONSIBILITY."
>
> -Eleanor Roosevelt

I woke up nervous, not knowing what to expect. I knew I was seeking justice for my son. The trial started two days before I was able to be present. God had been preparing me for this day over the last three years. I had been broken down to my core and knew that God was molding me into a different person. He was giving me strength. My life was changed forever. I knew I would never go back to being the timid, quiet, and naïve woman I had once been. She was gone, and I was a different person that was filled with intertwined pain, hurt, strength, and wisdom.

As I walked into the courtroom, I could see Charlie's mother and uncle to the right of me, along with his other family members. I could see the disgusted looks on some of the family members' faces, and I could hear someone smacking their lips. The whispers grew as I walked to take my seat at the front bench alongside my family. I couldn't believe the stares and looks I was receiving, as if I had done something wrong. Charlie had murdered our son and tried to murder me, but I guess I was supposed to overlook his behavior. Charlie had abused me in the past and had not been held accountable, and I'd thought that he would change. It was a hard lesson that cost me in the end. I usually try to see the good in everyone, but this was inexcusable. I felt like they were defending him or did not know how to react to this situation. Whatever it was, I could not believe that some of his family members were in this courtroom defending a murderer, even his pastor. I thought God said, "Thou shalt not kill." I guess they had missed the memo. I was so angry. I could not believe the eye rolls and the dirty looks I received. I thought I was in the twilight zone. This was just as unreal as the family members that attended the funeral walking past me, hugging his mother, and disregarding me. It was as if I was not grieving the death of my son; he was their family member as well. I was finally able to see the reality of how some people felt about the situation. It was sad to see their thought processes. I felt like my son's life was disregarded by some of the people there, and they were defending Charlie. The trial went on for four days, two of which I could not attend.

It is not what happens to you...It's how you let it affect you...You can fight or fold.

[UncleMo]

After that first day in court, I went home in disbelief over what I had witnessed. I know family is family, but I also know that right is right and wrong is wrong. It seemed to me as if my son was not a part of their family, and the only thing that mattered at that point was Charlie. I had to calm myself down and get ready for the next day. As I prepared, I looked at my picture on the wall that said, "I can do all things through Christ that strengthens me." (Philippians 3:15, New King James Version, NKJV.) That night my brother and I had an argument about my faith, but one thing that stuck with me was that he said, while you are looking at that scripture on the wall, you need to tap into your faith in God. He said that if you don't believe in the words, take that scripture off the wall because you do not have any faith. That really put a fire inside of me, knowing that if God was for me, who could be against me?

I walked into the courtroom again the next day and received the same looks and stares, but I noticed some family members were not there. The judge called me up to the stand to testify. As I sat down, my palms were sweaty, and I was so nervous because I had never been in this situation before. I knew I had to be strong for my son. I kept telling myself, Don't break down don't break down. I began to talk, and when the judge asked me to point to the person in the courtroom who had committed a crime against me, I pointed to Charlie. I described him along with what he was wearing: a tan shirt and pants that were provided by the jail. I could hear once again the smacking of the lips from his side of the family. I knew what I had to do regardless of their feelings. The judge asked for my highest level of education. I was proud to say master's degree, because, although I went through this traumatic experience, I knew that no one, not even Charlie, could break me.

I was on the stand, and I was asked various questions by my attorney and the public defender. I described the scene. I could see by the judge's face that he was outdone by all the evidence. I walked back to my seat and just stared Charlie down, nearly burning a hole in him. I hated him and was filled with anger. He never looked my way. I wanted him to know that I was no longer that scared, timid girl. I saw the smirk on his face, and that made my blood boil even more. How could this man whom I had once loved be so heartless? This was not the person that I had met years ago. Why, why, why? was all I could think. As I sat in my seat, I heard the additional testimonies, which included Officer Scott's. I even heard testimonies from people in my neighborhood that I had never known. The nurse eventestified about how, during Charlie's time in the hospital, he had admitted to killing our son and attempting to kill me. The nurse stated that he had been coherent and had known what he was saying. He was not on any medications that would make him drowsy.

After all the testimonies, we had a chance to speak out and let the judge know our feelings about the death of my son. I wanted justice to be served for my son as well as myself. After my mother and I presented our statements, Charlie's family went on the stand. Charlie's uncle was speaking on behalf of the family. According to court documentation, he initially stated that they did not condone the killing of Jaivon or the defendant's "horrific attack" and extended their sympathy to the family. He expressed the family's pain at the loss of Jaivon and stated that they were "appalled by this atrocity." He further stated that the family was certain that there were circumstances that contributed to the "intense evil and dark act" committed by the defendant. He explained that the defendant had lost one brother to gang violence, another to suicide, and his father to cancer. Charlie had difficulty adjusting to the loss, suffered "acute depression," and was advised by family members to seek counseling. Charlie's uncle characterized him as a caring young man with goals and dreams who was taught Christian values and respect for others. Charlie was employed until he became too depressed to effectively work during the six months prior to the murder and lost his ability to handle the everyday stresses of life. The family requested that Charlie be placed where he would receive psychological treatment so that he could remit his actions with rehabilitation and in some way prevent others from going to a deep place of depression and rage.

At this point I knew I was in the twilight zone. All I could hear was that, although he had raped and tried to kill me and later murdered his own son, he was suffering a lot and needed rehabilitation. Pretty much forget my son and his death but help Charlie. I was outraged! At that moment I hated Charlie, to be honest, and anyone else that did not see this as a problem. How dare they get on that stand and say something like that? People tried to paint this picture of who Charlie had been before. Evidently this was not the person he was today, so why even speak about it?

I was suffering from depression too. He had murdered our son, but did you see me trying to kill someone? How could they try to put that out as an explanation for this situation? There were not any words that could explain his actions. It really took me by surprise that a man of the cloth could propose this. This was one of those times where less would have been best. It was beyond depression. Charlie had an evil spirit in him. Regardless of all that, my focus was on Jaivon. At this point I was angry, and I was like, forget about everyone who is not for my son Jaivon. The ultimate goal was to seek justice for my son. I did not care how people looked at or thought of me.

The medical examiner described the cut to Jaivon's neck as a gaping wound that was four inches long by one and a half inches wide and one inch deep. The medical examiner also found that Jaivon had suffered numerous stabs and incised wounds to his back, chest, shoulders, left arm, and right leg. The medical examiner stated that Jaivon's throat was slit, and his head was decapitated from his body. The report stated that Jaivon lay on the floor choking on his own blood, gurgling to breathe, but was too full of blood and died. So after all of this, that Charlie's uncle could make a statement like that was appalling, and I was in disbelief.

After all the statements, it was time for the judge to make a ruling. Charlie received natural life in prison plus twenty-five years. This meant that he would never get out; I was overjoyed. I had waited all these years to receive justice for my son after he continued to plead not guilty and show no remorse for his actions. Only after I went out of the courtroom and into the hallway did I burst into tears. I was strong for the entire court case. I did not want Charlie to see me break down at all. I was crying profusely when the newspaper reporter asked me my feeling about the case. I stated that I was happy that justice had been served for Jaivon. That day was extremely emotional and overwhelming. I was overjoyed but also heartbroken because of my son's death. Charlie was still alive, but he had murdered our son, which was permanent and could not be reversed. In spite of justice being served, I missed my son.

God Will Humble You
To Prepare You For His Blessings

"YOU WILL BE BLESSED THE MOMENT
YOU REALIZE YOU ALREADY ARE."

-Bryant McGill

After graduating and finally receiving justice for my son, I was trying to figure out what my next steps would be. I was on cloud nine. I had my master's degree; I was ready to start my new journey, but I knew I had to find employment. I was still living with my parents, and I needed to move out and try to be on my own again. I realized that this time I would be all alone. I knew that this would be a scary process, but until then, I needed to find employment and fast. Several months went by, and I could not find employment. I went to multiple job interviews that stated I needed to have experience. I did not understand why, even though I had received my degrees and completed two internships, I still could not find employment.

My friend asked me if I wanted to work at a retail store with her, but I declined the offer, because I really wanted to find something in the social work profession. She asked me again, and once again I declined the offer and continued to look for employment in social work. I was determined to find employment, and with my degree, it should have been easy, right? That is what you would think, but it was not. I had received numerous no's from multiple employers, and I was becoming frustrated. I thought the goal was to get your degree, and then—boom— you would get employment. If only it was that simple.

I was becoming discouraged and depressed in addition to dealing with post- traumatic stress and anxiety from all the trauma that I had encountered. While waiting on employment, I received a call from the Section 8 housing office. I had applied when my son was first born and completely forgotten about it. I was excited because this would allow me to start the process of being on my own and regaining my independence. I was becoming desperate, so I decided to take my friend up on that previous offer to work in retail. She only had part-time openings, so I took it, but the store was an hour away from me. I was terrified of the expressway and took the street routes everywhere. It took forever to get to my destination, but I always made it.

I have come to realize that sometimes God must humble you to prepare you for his blessings and the next steps. I had worked in retail when I was in college, and I was back to where I originally started. I was working with my friends, just like old times. I came to realize that, although I had the degrees, it was still challenging to find employment and that you had to be grateful for what you had so that God could bless you with more. I was still in the process of searching for full-time employment in the social work profession, and I was looking for an apartment as well. I wanted to live near my parents, who had stayed in a diverse community, so that I could check up on them. I was terrified to be alone. I knew that it was time for me to walk by faith and not by sight, knowing that I would not be alone and that God would be there every step of the way.

It was a struggle, because I was only working fifteen hours a week, and the landlords in that area were not accepting Section 8 participants. I felt discriminated against. I was being rejected for employment within my profession because of my lack of experience and finding affordable housing in a nice area. I thought it would be easy to find housing, but I realized that many people had a negative stigma or Preconception about Section 8 recipients. Some assumed that people who received Section 8 housing services were lazy or not looking for work, but that was not true. I was a prime example. I had three degrees and was actively looking for better employment but needed assistance to reach my goals. I was grateful that I received the voucher when I did because it really helped me transition into independence. People should not place a stigma on others, because they never know a person's story. It seemed like I was looking for an apartment for months, but after four months, I was finally able to find one. My mom decided to reach out to her old landlord. He had a great property that was blocks away from them. I was so happy! I was exhausted after being told no so many times, but I had finally received a yes! I was finally moving into my own apartment and starting fresh. I had the apartment, and now it was time for me to find employment. I knew that God was in control and was going to help me get a new position. I just needed to keep the faith.

I applied for a temp job, and I also applied to work as a correctional officer at a penitentiary. My youngest brother was working there, and he always had great jobs that paid well, so I was trying to make some money to live. I was trying to figure it out. I was tired of asking my parents for assistance and wanted to get back up on my feet. I continued to work at the shoe store, and I finally received a call back from the temp agency to work at Catholic Charities as a caseworker. The good part was that I would have employment in my profession, but I wouldn't have any benefits until I was hired full time. I felt like I was finally moving forward. I started working at Catholic Charities that same month and provided the shoe store with a two-week notice. I was excited about working at Catholic Charities, because I knew that I would be assisting clients to reach their goals. It seemed like a dream come true. I enjoyed working for this organization, and I felt like I was making a great impact on my clients. I was three months into this position when I received a call from the penitentiary asking me if I wanted the job of correctional officer.

I was nervous, but I spoke to my brother and weighed my options. I said yes. Little did I know that this experience would change my life forever for the better.

Next

"IT IS NOT THE BRUISES ON THE BODY THAT HURT. IT IS THE WOUNDS OF THE HEART AND THE SCARS ON THE MIND."

-Aisha Mirza

I remember my first day going into the penitentiary, which happened to be an all-male maximum-security facility. I pulled up in my 2007 silver Chevy Malibu and parked next to this other car driven by a young man who was dressed up. I guess we were going to the same place, and although I wasn't dressed up, I asked him where he was going all dressed up.

He said that he was starting the job as well. I hadn't gotten the memo about the dress code; I had on some jeans and a hoody. He caught my attention because he looked handsome, but I couldn't focus on that now. I was trying to get over my nerves. I was trying to decipher what I had gotten myself into. The veteran correctional officers gave us a tour of the facility. I was even more nervous than before. I'm not going to lie—I was scared. I could hear echoes of other correctional officers in the hallway saying, "Aww— look at the rookies." I was scared out of my mind, and here came people talking about looking at the rookies. While on the tour, we were guided to a cell house called F House, or Round House. It was a large, round room full of cells. All I could hear was yelling and banging on the doors throughout the entire cell house. At this point I was extremely scared, but I tried to put on a brave face like I was not terrified by what I heard and saw. I was ready to run out of the job. I didn't know what to expect, but there was no turning back at this point. I was tired of being broke and needed this job, so I decided to stick it out. This was a long way from my previous profession in social work/case work from the looks of it. It was difficult finding employment within my profession, and this could be a stepping stone. At the end of the shift, the group of new correctional officers walked to the area to have our photo taken. It was awkward, because I didn't know whether to smile or not. I had not thought about it before, but at that moment, I realized that this profession was out of my comfort zone.

I started at the Department of Corrections Academy and didn't know what to expect there either. This was all new territory. I was taken aback when I arrived at the academy; it was like boot camp. I was not used to this; I was used to an office environment where I would enjoy dressing up and doing paperwork. My first day at the academy, I thought, would be like an introduction to my new career choice and what would be expected in the role of a corrections officer.

I got a rude surprise. As soon as we made it to the academy, all I could hear from the lieutenant was "This is not a game. When you get off the bus, you need to run to the doorway. If you are lacking, there will be consequences." What was this? I gathered my large, black luggage bag and begin to run as fast as I could to the academy doors. Once I got inside, I heard, "Dump everything on the gym floor." I couldn't believe they were serious, but they were. The directors began to check each person's bag, making sure no contraband was found, as if we were inmates.

I was exhausted. My fresh sew-in was dismantled, and my leave-out was now frizzy from running. I had to wrap my mind around the fact that I had gone from cute outfits to hot combat boots. The early mornings of eating nasty food and being told what to do were a lot to take in. My days there consisted of participating in self-defense sessions, shooting, sitting in classroom trainings, sleeping, and getting up to do it all over again. If one person messed up on a drill or talked out of turn, we had to do push-ups—from twenty to fifty or more. I was exhausted, but I knew it would be worth it. I called my brother, because he had already been through the training process. I cried, saying, "I can't do this! It is too hard." He said to man up. In my sad voice, I said, "I am a woman." We were being told when to sleep, use the phone, eat—everything felt like boot camp. I had to learn how to shoot a gun; I had never shot a weapon before. It was exciting and stressful at the same time for me, and I failed shooting at the range the first time. If I didn't pass, I was out of a job. This was what they hadn't told me. I had already quit my job; I could not afford to be without employment again. I needed this job, and bad.

I could not believe I had failed the range. I went home and went to the gun range with my brother and his friend. Normally my brother and I are kind of distant, but working in this profession gave us a way to bond. I was happy to be establishing a closer relationship with him, and I could tell he was proud of me. My family was proud of the woman that I was becoming. I went back to the range the next week and passed the test, but next was physical training. In that training was the guy I had met in the parking lot on the first day; his name was Chris. I was smitten with him because, when I had to run and was falling behind, he came up and encouraged me to keep going. I had not really talked to or liked anyone in a long time; my whole world consisted of the trial and school. I did not go outside much and wasn't trying to be with anyone. I was working on healing and becoming a better me. Chris and his charm took me by surprise. I noticed that he was a flirt, but I didn't care; I wanted him. I also met a close friend in the academy, Amanda. Overall, we had a good group. The final day arrived— graduation day. My family was present as they called my name; I was not the same person I'd been when I'd come to the academy. I was able to challenge myself and tap into my resilience to complete this training. At that point I felt that if I could survive almost being murdered and losing my child, I could do anything.

After the academy it was time to go to the institution, and I did not know what to expect once again. I was going to be around murderers, rapists, and any other type of criminal you could think of. I was afraid of this new venture that God had for me, but I was there, and I could not turn back now. I had my classmates with me from the academy. We helped each other and stuck together. It was a good feeling to know that you had people that had your back.

I had my close friend and Chris. We all established a close relationship and became great friends. I liked him a lot, but he only looked at me as a friend. I hoped I could change his mind. Many women found the same characteristics appealing and were attracted to him. I felt a certain way about him talking to other women, but what could I do? I would hang out with Chris after work. I even went to a couple of his family events. I was hoping that it would eventually evolve, and it could be something more and I could not understand why he didn't want me. What was wrong with me? Was I not pretty enough? I did not have a large butt; maybe that was it. I understand now that if someone doesn't want to be in a relationship with you, then you cannot make them. I realized I needed to work on self- love and self-worth. I was dealing with a tremendous amount of hurt from my son's death and my past relationship. Still, I wanted Chris to feel the way I felt about him. After years I had finally opened my heart to someone, only to be rejected. I needed to go back to therapy to deal with unresolved issues.

Meanwhile at work it was a different arena, and I had to lock up inmates, get them out of the cell, and perform additional duties. This was a long way from social work and conducting home visits. It was like social work but in a different light, and I was still hopeful that I could make a difference. I remember being in a unit where it was full of noise, yelling, and banging on doors. I was not used to this type of behavior, but I learned how to adjust from the person I considered my work dad. Dave taught me the ropes and how to be a successful correctional officer. He was truly a blessing.

I was working on the day shift for a year and then got bumped to the night shift with my brother. This was the closest that my brother and I had ever been; we formed a bond. Even though it was formed in a penitentiary, this bond between us will forever be in my memories and heart. All I ever wanted was for my brothers to be proud of me and not look at me with disappointment. I felt like I had already taken the family through enough. I just wanted them to be proud of me for something. I was working in an environment that, if you had told me five years ago I would be working there, I would never have believed you. I felt like God had placed me in this position to know that he had my back through everything.

Chris and I never evolved, but I decided to remove myself from the situation, because when I love, I love hard. I could not deal with the feeling of being rejected by him and with him talking to other women. I talked to other people, but if Chris had stated he wanted to be with me, I would have been with him. I have a better understanding and have grown to realize that everyone has a role in a person's life, and sometimes it can be for a friendship and not a romantic relationship. I guess, after the trauma, I just wanted someone to love me, but ultimately, I needed to love myself. I was so broken and hurt, but finally realized that I had to work on me and heal before I could incorporate anyone into my life. During this experience I was able to conceptualize various factors about myself. I was able to have a stronger relationship with my brother. I was able to grow mentally, work on my spiritual journey, and learn how to love myself and become the queen that I am. I realized that yearning and searching for love in others had to start with loving myself and knowing my worth. I had to learn to accept the value of one's words and not read between the lines. I decided to start another position as a caseworker that would allow me to grow professionally. I kept thinking to myself that this was a tough journey, but I had come, I had seen, and I had conquered the position of correctional officer. It was now time for me to work on becoming a better me.

My Spiritual Metamorphosis

"MENTAL HEALTH IS NOT A DESTINATION, BUT A PROCESS. IT'S ABOUT HOW YOU DRIVE, NOT WHERE YOUR'RE GOING."

-Noam Shpancer

The time of searching for myself was really challenging. I was told different things by my therapist that I did not want to hear about my mental health. After the traumatic event, sometimes I would seclude myself from everyone and did not want to get out of bed. I would even skip events because I was feeling horrible even though I looked fine on the outside. Sometimes I was just dying inside grieving and still trying to conceptualize that I would never see my son get older. I could only imagine how it would feel looking at my nephew and nieces as they grew. I would wonder how my son would have fit in with the kids and what he would like to do. I continued to pray and ask God for his guidance to keep me.

Many people attempt to disregard mental health, but it is important. Accepting my challenges and dealing with certain issues was the first stage of healing. I had to accept my flaws, start there, and move forward. Sometimes I stillgot stuck in the past. I was allowing past things to control my future.

It was extremely difficult to date, and it continues to be a primary issue. I had become so numb to people going in and out of my life that I could not get my hopes up that any relationship would work. It seemed like I had a pattern of trying to establish relationships with men who were not interested in me. They would prefer to have sex without any commitment, and I felt that was unacceptable.

During this time, I became sick and thought that it was a common cold, but in all actuality, there was a spiritual metamorphosis taking place. The doctors were unable to tell me what exactly was wrong with me and continued to guess. I had shortness of breath and other symptoms that I could not figure out. I may have had covid 19. I was prescribed various medications and was unable to eat and lost weight. I was already thin and did not want to lose any additional weight, but I could not eat. My entire face broke out. I was miserable and wanted to feel better. I had a couple of people that would check on me; one, in particular, checked on me every day. I was grateful for his presence during this difficult time. He passed away a few months later, but it was a blessing to speak to him during this time frame. His death made me realize that life is too short, and we never know when we will leave this earth.

This made me examine myself and realize that there was not a living person who could help me. I could pray to God, hoping that I would be heard. It was only God and me. This was the time that God had been waiting for. During my daily life schedule, I was too busy and often did not fit God into my schedule. I know that sounds bad, but we often get so wrapped up in our own world that we may forget. I feel like this was God's way of sitting me down to talk to me. I was crying out, "God, heal me" and "God, help me." I didn't know what was wrong with me. No one could hear me or know what I was going through. I felt like I was going crazy, because I wanted to feel better, and no one could be around me. Oftentimes we take our health and life for granted and do not realize it can be taken away in the blink of an eye. This experience was definitely an eye-opener, and I contemplated many things. I felt like God was cleansing me through this phase of sickness and increasing my faith to lean on him. As I entered a new chapter in my life, I began to have a different awakening and view on life. I realized that we are not only fighting a physical battle, but a spiritual battle in life which can affect us in different ways. "Let your light so shine that men will see your good works and acknowledge your father in heaven" (Matthew 5:14).

Loving Me

"YOUR RELATIONSHIP WITH YOURSELF SETS THE TONE FOR EVERY OTHER RELATIONSHIP YOU HAVE."

-Robert Holden

Thinking back, I know I had to finally put God first in my life and begin to love myself. I was looking for validation and acceptance in past relationships and situation- ships because I did not love myself. I was hurting, and that was keeping me from looking at things I needed to work on within myself. I realize that I allowed certain things to take place in my life, but I needed to put myself first. I now understand that people can only treat you a certain way if you allow them. It took me a long time of being isolated and becoming ill to begin to see the bigger picture and search for a way to start loving myself.

As stated earlier, I had been sick for three months, not knowing what was wrong with me. I felt like I was going to die. I prayed and asked God to help me through whatever it was I was going through. At this point God was the only one there for me, and I could hear his voice subconsciously. This was the first time in many years that I was able to sit with my thoughts and feelings. I could not run or create a blockage by being busy so that I would not have to think and deal with my hurt and pain. This experience allowed me to increase my faith, and I know that I have been able to get to where I am currently due to God's grace.

Upon crying out to God, I began to see the ugly truths within myself. I was still hurting and needed to heal. God revealed the woman that others probably saw, but I did not realize how broken and hurt I was, which I often tried to cover up. I would conceal my hurt with clothes, with makeup, and with a smile of happiness, but overall I was in pain and didn't know how to deal with it. I saw the hurting woman and wondered why relationships would not work out. I attracted others who were hurting, and we would bond in our pain, which never led to anything healthy. I had to realize that, in order to be in a successful and healthy relationship, I had to look deep inside myself and begin doing the work of healing from within.

I began on my journey of healing by putting God first in my life and by praying and learning to love myself. I would listen to positive affirmations and music that had a positive message that blocked out negativity. I started to eat differently, exercise, and read my Bible and attend church. I also began to help others, such as feeding people who were less fortunate. I forgave myself for not loving and for neglecting myself. I walked away from things that were not pleasing to GOD and prevented my growth into the woman that God had created me to be. I am not perfect and am still learning how to love myself.

I am more self-aware and understand that sometimes people are only in your life for a season, and I am learning to be comfortable with this. Everyone is not meant to be in our lives forever. People are often sent to teach us a lesson— either good or bad. I have learned to live with both and apply the lessons in each situation to make me become a better person. I'm still working on loving me in hope of finding my ultimate love, which is within myself.

You Are A Depiction of Your Tomorrow

"LEARN FROM YESTERDAY,
LIVE FOR TODAY,
HOPE FOR TOMORROW."

-Albert Einstein

I had been blessed by the people who were there for me during this time. I began to take the time out to reflect on what I could do to create a change in this world. I was reflecting on how I could keep my son's memory alive. If I were to die today, I would want to leave a legacy. What was my purpose? How could

147

I reach my goals? How could I become a better me? During this time many thoughts were going through my head. I just knew that I did not want to leave this earth without creating a change. I was battling with my physical health but also my mental health. Usually, I overloaded myself with so many tasks that I never had a chance to think about everything that had taken place in my life and how it had affected me. The hurt and pain that I had endured caused me to express myself in other ways. I was looking for someone to love me, and I placed my hurt into finding someone. I ultimately needed to sit down with God and start healing. I was able to think, which was painful. I felt like God was resetting my mind and helping me to heal. I am working every day to become a better person, but I am still human and fall short at times. I feel like we are like puzzle pieces and are created and designed to help each other to fulfill our purpose. This pandemic has taken many people's lives and has shown the evilness of this world. Racial tensions and killings and just pure evils have come over this world. We must remember that God is love and the overall factor in our lives.

I'm learning every day and praying that I can encourage and help someone overcome through my life story. I can't wait to see what happiness the future holds.

To be continued...

Only God 365

"THOSE WHO HOPE IN THE LORD
WILL RENEW THEIR STRENGTH."

Isaiah 40:31

It is only by the grace of God that I am still alive today. Looking back on the whole ordeal, I don't even know how I made it through. The only thing I can think of is that it had to be God. Many people would have lost their minds after going through such a traumatic situation, resorting to drugs, alcohol, or another coping mechanism, but I am still making it through. I'm getting stronger each and every day and am compelled to help others even through my pain. I feel like I am here to provide a message and let people know that God is real. Many people may believe in a higher existence, but I believe in God. There is definitely a spiritual realm beyond this world; that is what I believe.

I began to have multiple dreams of my son letting me know that he was okay. In addition to the dreams, I was having strange encounters. I was in my car, and the locks began to go up and down by themselves. I was the only one in the car and was not touching anything but the steering wheel. I felt like this had to be my son, because this was the place where we spent most of our time, from driving to my mother's house to speech therapy, etc. As the locks continued to go up and down, I told my son to go with Jesus. We would pray every night when he was alive, and I would tell him to pray to Jesus. After two minutes the locks began to subside, and it never happened again. My baby was gone. I felt helpless, and the only thing

I could say was "Go to God," because my son was not here with me in his physical form. As I stated earlier, I was lost during this time frame and did not know what to do or how to live without Jaivon. God has kept me and is continuing to keep me. I hope this book is a blessing to someone and that my son is never forgotten.

In Loving Memory of Jaivon

Resources

> "KNOWLEDGE IS POWER."
>
> -Francis Bacon

National Domestic Violence Hotline: (800) 799-7233 or (800) 787-3224 TTY, thehotline.org

loveisrespect: (866) 331-9474 or text "loveis" to 22522, loveisrespect

National Center on Elder Abuse: (855) 500-3537, ncea-info@aoa.hhs.gov

National Suicide Prevention Lifeline: (800) 273-8255

LGBT National Hotline: (888) 843-4564

National Alliance on Mental Illness (NAMI) Helpline: (800) 950-6264

Let You Journey Begin

"I AM LEARNING TO TRUST THE JOURNEY
EVEN WHEN I DO NOT UNDERSTAND IT."

-Mila Bron

MARGARET JEFFERSON

_____

_____

_____

_____

_____

_____

_____

_____

_____

_____

_____

_____

_____

_____

_____

_____

_____

_____

_____

_____

_____

_____

_____

_____

_____

_____

_____

_____

_____

_____

_____

_____

_____

_____

_____

_____

_____

MARGARET JEFFERSON

_____

_____

_____

_____

_____

_____

_____

_____

_____

_____

_____

_____

_____

_____

_____

_____

_____

_____

_____

_____

_____

_____

_____

_____

_____

_____

_____

_____

_____

_____

_____

_____

_____

_____

_____

_____

_____

_____

_____

_____

_____

_____

_____

_____

_____

_____

_____

_____

_____

_____

_____

_____

_____

_____

_____

_____

_____

_____

_____

_____

_____

_____

MARGARET JEFFERSON

_____

_____

_____

_____

_____

_____

_____

_____

_____

_____

_____

_____

_____

_____

_____

_____

_____

_____

_____

_____

_____

_____

_____

_____

_____

About The Author

"SHE WAS POWERFUL, NOT BECAUSE SHE WASN'T SCARED BUT BECAUSE SHE WENT ON SO STRONGLY DESPITE THE FEAR."

-Atticus

Margaret Jefferson was born in Chicago, Illinois, and grew up in the Austin Community on the West side of the city. Despite facing financial challenges at times, she had the support of both her parents, as well as the love and encouragement of her family and friends. From a young age, she was instilled with the importance of faith and knowing God. On November 9, 2007, she gave birth to her first and only child, "Jaivon." Her life took a deeply unfortunate turn when her son later lost his life due to Intimate Partner Violence (IPV) or Domestic Violence. This devastating event profoundly changed Margaret's life, leading her to lean on her faith in God even more. She grappled with confusion and uncertainty about her purpose in the wake of this tragedy.

Margaret had a deep passion for learning, which served as an escape from her harsh reality. She pursued her education diligently, earning a bachelor's degree in social work (BSW) in Chicago, IL, and later a master's degree in social work (MSW), graduating with honors. Her dedication and commitment to addressing issues of violence against women earned her the Violence Against Women Act Award (VAWA) from the former Mayor and State's Attorney. Margaret has since become a powerful advocate, using her own story to raise awareness and speak out against IPV and DV. She has shared her experiences at various events, including the UIC 25th Homicide Victim Memorial, Concert for America, National Coalition Against Domestic Violence, and many others. Her goal is to offer hope and inspiration to others by sharing her truth.

Currently, Margaret is working on writing books that aim to uplift and empower individuals to find their purpose. She is also in the process of establishing a resource center in Chicago's Austin neighborhood. Her passion is to be a beacon of light for those in dark places by sharing her personal journey. Margaret finds healing and fulfillment in speaking out about her past traumas, and she sees it as a way to give back to others. Her family and friends describe her as a true blessing in their lives, noting her unwavering dedication to making a positive difference in society.

MARGARET JEFFERSON

www.ingramcontent.com/pod-product-compliance
Lightning Source LLC
Chambersburg PA
CBHW051515120626
46551CB00012B/930